VIEW FROM THE
SECOND ROW

VIEW FROM THE SECOND ROW

Through the Eyes of First Lady,

Evangelist Rockell Y. Williams Brown

Rockell Y. Williams Brown

To order additional copies of this book, contact:
Xlibris Corporation
1-888-795-4274
www.Xlibris.com
Orders@Xlibris.com
61228

CONTENTS

Write the vision, and make it plain upon tables, that he may run that reads it.—Habakkuk 2:2

The Lord gave the word: great was the company of those that published it.—Psalms 68:11

BIOGRAPHY

Rockell Y. Williams Brown was born in Anchovy, a lush mountainous village seven miles south of Montego Bay, Jamaica, to Ruth and Victor Williams who are now deceased. Rockell is the fifth of their eight children. Rockell attended public schools in New York city, and after graduation from High School she attended the City University of New York for two years. There she studied liberal arts where intellectual capability was stimulated. She has earned two college degrees: the first from the Institute of Business Management in 1981 with major in business law, the second a Professional Paralegal Degree in 1994, with specialty in Real Estate Law. Rockell has been a Paralegal for 28 years with attention given to the area of Real Property Law in Community Government. Throughout Rockell life she has been placed in positions which compelled her to write and which contributed significantly to the present authorship of her first published book, *"View From The Second Row"*. As a child, Rockell was taught that decent young women should not be too chatty. Cultural stronghold led her to internalize her point of views so as pastime, she wrote short stories and essays for her pleasure. Many years after marriage, she began to journal religiously, this as she said, lightened her spiritual awareness. Still, it never occurred to Rockell that she could become a published writer. Rockell writes study manuals for the ministry where her husband Rev, Barrington E. Brown is the Pastor. She writes articles for the church newsletter as well as proposals for grants. When Rockell is not working as a Paralegal in her busy office in Florida, she spends her time as Co-Pastor with her husband, teaching several classes including Adult Bible Studies, Women in Ministry Classes, New Membership Preparedness class, etc. Barrington and Rockell are Founders and Pastors of Poinciana Pentecostal Church of God, in Kissimmee Florida.

To my husband Barrington, in dedication to your tender heart, your words of wisdom and your kind smile for everyone—I love you. Without your patience, understanding and support, and most of all love, the completion of this work would not have been possible. I dedicate this book to my parents, and my Sister Robin, whose memory will live on in me perpetually; to my brothers and sisters, Peter, Dean, Stead, Colleen, Charmaine and Janice, I love you all dearly. To my children, Dwayne, Wayne, and Tristan, remember that I will always love you, and to my grand-daughters Anissa and Nyeimah, you are my heart.

I love you all.

And I am sure that he who began a good work in you will complete it.
—Philippians 1:6

CHAPTER ONE

Sunday Morning

"But when He, the Spirit of truth, comes, He will guide you into all truth. He will not speak on his own; He will speak only what He hears, and He will tell you what is yet to come."—John 16:13

It's Sunday morning once again. The choir prepares itself for the procession. Before the final call to devotion, the ushers and greeters are busy having the people who come for the morning worship service seated. Some deacons are still on the outdoors, directing motorists and those who are hurrying in to find a good space to park on the church grounds. Mothers with their crying babies and young children proceed to the far back pews. Prayer warriors are still seen in an attitude of prayer as they exit the Prayer room to go into the sanctuary before the procession. Sometimes if they are really late in coming out Pastor will knock on the closed door to allow them to join us in on the procession.

So here I am just standing there in quiet observation, taking in as much as I can. I can see hats of many shapes and sizes and color. Dresses, suits and ties are brought together in such fit to be seen coordination. I especially love to see the two year old baby girls who have graduated from baby clothes to pretty little pastel dresses just because they can now walk on their own. Of course, they must come over for their hugs.

Before the procession the choir echoes their usual anthem, "We've Come This Far By Faith". In the distance, I hear the music director inviting the congregation to stand to receive the Pastor and the Ecclesiastical body. So I position myself behind the pastor, my husband and co-worker in the ministry, that I can take my weekly walk down the center aisle of the church. As we proceed down the aisle, led by the choir, my eyes have no recourse but to make contact with many onlookers who have already stood singing. Some would smile with me, because as First Lady, I am expected to have a smile at all times. As I pass the congregants, there are those who would wave to me as I breathe a whisper "hello" or I wave back. Sometimes I may make a gesture of "good to see you again." Other times, I find myself joining in with an uplifting voice, ending the stanza. Because I so love to sing, I'll join in on the note, "Leaning on the Lord."

Each Sunday morning I prepare my heart for a time of spiritual renewal. I put myself in a frame of mind just so I may enter in the presence of the Lord. It's a time and place where I meet God, and He meets me. My focus is tuning everything and everybody out so as to reflect on Jesus and how He has changed my life and has blessed me. Because my Bible say to me to forsake not the assembling of ourselves together [*Hebrews 10:25*] I look forward for each Sunday morning when I can worship again with my church brothers and sisters. So many times I find myself caught up in the spirit of awe, as I continue in the procession behind Pastor to my assigned seat on the "Second Row". There, I kneel in reverence to give thanks to God because it is He who has brought me this far by faith. I always thought before and now I know, that I am not my own, I belong to Jesus. He gave His life for me on Calvary, to save me from my unrighteousness, so how can I let Him down. There have been so many obstacles, shame and disgrace and much pain that have risen up in my life beyond what I can bear. There have been stumbling blocks too. Sometimes when I try so hard to serve the Lord, that is when the enemy begins his attacks on me. He tries with my finances, my family, my marriage, my health, and whatever kind of fiery darts he can find to throw my way. It is then that I realize that it is not me that he is fighting. It is me that he is using. He wants me to fail and become discouraged so that the Pastor will fail, so that God's work will fail, so that he can have victory. But the Bible reminds me over and over again, that "No weapon that is formed against me shall prosper". Isaiah 54:17. The devil is already defeated because he was cast out of heaven.

Far so many times we go to church for reasons other than to meet Jesus. We have all kinds of ulterior motives. Sometimes we go to church because we were made as youngsters to go with our parents. We go to church out of routine and tradition. We go to church because we like or infatuated with the Pastor, or we like his preaching techniques or we like the different programs that are being offered there. We go because we enjoy the music. Some even go to be entertained. We go because of the architecture. My God! These are all carnal motives. Our intent should not be based upon what is happening around us but rather upon Jesus Christ and His love for us. Why then must we go to church simply because we personally want something from the programs offered in any Ministry? One man even told me that he is looking for a wife who owns a home and a have a good job. Well no one was interested in him because of his arrogance, so he later moved on to another church. Another boycotted the church and said she would not give an offering unless she receives a personal call from the pastor. Another said she would not return because the pastor wife stared at her, and she felt uncomfortable. Another said that someone did not shake her hand during the fellowship time and she is offended. To me I believe those are selfish motives. Proverbs 3 verse 5 reminds me that we must "Trust in the Lord with all our heart, and lean not on our own understanding, but in all our ways, acknowledge Him, and he will direct our path." We should also delight ourselves also in the Lord, and he will grant us the desires of our heart. Psalm 37: 4. So many times we fail to remember that God loves us so much so that He gave us His one and only Son. John 3:16. That's why I thank Him. That's why I Worship Him. Many times we fail to recognize that it is not about us. It's about Jesus. That's why Sunday mornings is a time of hope and expectation for me. It's a time when God's presence dwells among us individually and collectively. In the days of Moses according to Exodus 40, we read of how the glory of the Lord filled the tabernacle. "The cloud covered the tabernacle even in the clearest day; it was not a cloud which the sun scatters. This cloud was a token of God's presence to be seen day and night, by all Israel, that they might never again question, Is the Lord among us, or is he not? It guided the camp of Israel through the wilderness. While the cloud rested on the tabernacle, they rested; when it removed, they followed it. The glory of the Lord filled the tabernacle. In light and fire the Shekhinah made itself visible: God is Light; our God is a consuming Fire. Yet so dazzling was the light, and so dreadful the fire, that Moses was not able to enter into the tent of the congregation, till the splendor was abated. But what Moses could not do, our Lord Jesus has done, whom God caused to draw near; and who has invited us to come boldly, even to the mercy-seat. Being taught by the Holy Spirit to follow the example of Christ, as well as to depend upon him, to attend his ordinances, and obey his precepts, we shall be kept from losing our way, and be led in the midst of the paths of judgment, till we come to heaven, the habitation of his holiness." (*Commentary-BibleGateway.com*)

This is why Sunday morning is a sacred time when I don't want to miss out on my blessing. I want to be there when God decides to pour out his spirit upon us. Shekhinah means the presence of the Lord. We are in the last days. Joel 2 said that in the last days God will pour our His spirit upon all flesh. So I want to be there when the water is troubled. I want to be there when his presence is manifested. That's why I kneel in reverence and wait before the King.

In certain moments my eyes would open and my focus would be set to the altar area of the Sanctuary. I see the choir in their robes singing praises to God. I see the musicians energetically playing their instrument. I am reminded of Psalm 150. What a splendor my eyes behold. The Pastor is seated; eyes closed with his palm closed as well, bearing up his chin. He is clothed in his pastorate vesture. His posture is that of one of authority. His head is tilted slightly in meditation as he listens to the praises. I love him but I love the Lord more, for He first loved me.

Just then, my thought rolls back to Isaiah 6 which describes the Lord seated high on His throne. The scripture said His train filled the temple. I visualized the cherubim and the seraphim all singing, "Holy, Holy, Holy". This is why I have a feeling of awe when I am in God's presence. At that point, my focus was interrupted as I listen to the Moderator announces that "It is time for Praise and Worship".

Worship time is a blessing to me. With prayer on my lips, I took the given opportunity to send up worship and praises to God. I personally reflect on my life, where I was and where I am now and where the Lord is leading me. As I look back over my life I can remember where the Lord has taken me from. I can remember myself as a child of no more than four years old. I now recall that it was then although quite young, that God had called me to ministry. I know now as a pastor's wife that it was not my doing but the Lords'.

CHAPTER TWO

My Calling

"But when He, the Spirit of truth, comes, He will guide you into all truth. He will not speak on his own; He will speak only what He hears, and He will tell you what is yet to come."—John 16:13

When I was about four or maybe five years old, my beautiful spirit filled mother whose memories I cherished dearly, introduced the Lord to me. She would gather my sisters and me in her bed at end of the day before we were tucked snuggly away underneath candlewick coverlets in our own little beds. This was to become a customary thing because it was there that I learned to read. Daddy wasn't there. I didn't know him. As I grew older I was told that our daddy was away in England. Momma would read Bible stories to us and as we the older ones learned to read better she would let us read the Bible out loud as well. I loved the "Big Bible" because of the beautiful pictures between the pages. Even though we made lots of mistakes, she lovingly corrected us, and made us repeat the mispronounced words over and over again until we got it right. I recall the large print-black covered family bible, which was always kept in the same place on lace doilies on a table strategically placed in a corner in the sitting room. A big vase of fresh lilies from the yard would always serve as an accent piece there as well. These lilies grow wild on the land we owned. Some pages of the Bible had pictures of Jesus and little lambs at his feet, some pictures were of angels protecting little children as they stumbled. All these things made browsing through the Bible very interesting when Momma read to us. Even more interesting was the fact that she took the time to explain what each picture meant. The unusual thing about one particular evening as I recall was that she taught us all how to pray. It wasn't odd for us all to kneel and repeat the Lord's Prayer as Momma had taught us, and then sing this little chorus, which I know my younger sisters still remember today. It goes, "*Jesus Christ in heaven I pray—guide me through each night and day. AMEN.*" Only now as a Christian I appreciate the fact that it was there and then that my mother has led us into the long established family devotion. She would tell us that the angel of the Lord encamped round about them that fear him. Only Momma would sometimes, not always, say it in the native dialect. "*Pickney unu hush-up nuh, God angels them is up-up on the house top." We mus be silent and sure that we prayers them a good wans, so that way, they can fly weh wid we prayers them and take dem to Jesus. If you good pickneys, Lord Jesas will take your prayers and will give you whatever yu ask fa. Hush-up, did unu hear the angels dem wings a fly weh?*" Not all times Momma would speak the dialect that they call patois though. Proper English was a must in our home, especially when we reached that impressionable age of learning. Although we understood it we were encouraged not to speak it.

I am so certain that I heard the wings of angels then. As I grew older, Momma had to go away to live in England. It was those thoughts which kept me, and as I continued to grown-up, I would actually see Angels in my dreams. One night as I slept, I saw in my dreams a holy being descending out of the sky and strategically appeared before me. His arms were outstretched. His feet never touched the ground. He was clothed in pure white apparel, and His hair was yellow gold. His hair was well arranged with no distinctive strand out of place. His eyes were blue. He had a smile which compellingly said "I am calling you. His arms were stretched towards me and only me. No one else was around but me. His fingers beckoned me to come close to him. I was not alarmed. I felt at peace.

I can still see His image even today, as though it happened just moments ago. I praise the Lord even more now because it was only when I gave my heart fully and completely to the Lord that He revealed to me the dream and spoke to my heart that He had a special call on my life. I so appreciate that dream. The Lord has called me, from a child. He watched me made mistakes; he saw my failures and my transgressions. Some, I am not proud of. He saw my heart, when I didn't even know that I had a heart. He saw my disappointments and my discouragements when I was in despondency. He saw my humility, when I didn't even know that I was being humble. He saw my patience, when I didn't even know yet that I was a tolerant person. He saw me even before I was formed in my mother's womb. Before I was born He set me apart and appointed me as First Lady over my husband's ministry. (Jeremiah 1:5—paraphrased). He saw me, because He was there when I was molded by His precious hands. You know what? He said "That's good". Ha!

So that's why He has placed a hedge around me, to protect me when my mother had left us, her young children, to migrate to England. When I wanted to reach out to the Lord, He brought back to my recollection that sacred and precious dream. I believe He was saying to me, "Ask anything of me in the name of My Son Jesus, and it shall be granted." "Go ahead! Ask of me and I shall give . . . . to you. Psalm 2: 8a; Matthew 7:7; Luke 11:9.

Now, I realize that because I feared the Lord, He was with me then and is always with me even now. When I walk through the valley of the shadow of death, (Psalm 23:4a) He was with me. I remember I was about nine years old when I was sick to death, with Aego Fever. But God was there with me. I had a sickness called Mumps. When I had another illness called Whooping Cough, He had never left me. I was sick again with something they called

Aegy fever. I looked it up on the Internet, and according to the *Answers. com* an online Encyclopedia my research found that Aegy fever another form of "*Dengue fever [**Aedes aegypti**] is a disease caused by one of a number of viruses that are carried by mosquitoes. These mosquitoes then transmit the virus to humans. The most common victims are children younger than 10 years of age. The virus that causes dengue fever is called an arbovirus, which stands for arthropod-borne virus. Mosquitoes are a type of arthropod. In a number of regions, mosquitoes carry this virus and are responsible for passing it along to humans. These regions include the Middle East, the Far East, Africa, and the Caribbean Islands*"—(end quote) Answers.com

It was bad because I was unable to raise my head or body from one position for like three days, maybe more. I do not know. I was in a state of minor paralysis. The fever was not letting up. I remembered old women tending to me. That's what I remembered. I recalled another time, I had another contagious disease called "Mumps", and another time I had Whooping Cough. Most of the children had some kinds of diseases or the other back then, but the Lord was with me. These were diseases which led to many fatalities during the early and mid 1960's. God was with me then and He is still with me now. He never left me. I left Him. There was a period of time in my life when I failed to stay before my Lord. I failed to pray. I failed to study. I failed to praise or worship Him. That was the times when I have allowed my flesh to be in control. I became disobedient, and rebellious. And yet that's the time when I cried the most because I felt so all alone and ashamed. Jesus didn't leave me. I left Him. I didn't know why. But that's how the devil works. He makes you walk in the big, bright and beautiful paths, to destroy you in the end. But when I would think of Jesus again and all the things that He has done for me, How He kept me through childhood illnesses, I cried out loud to the Lord once again to forgive me as I earnestly repented of my transgressions. I am reminded again and again as He speaks to me through His word saying, daughter, "Fear thou not;

for I am with thee: Be not dismayed; for I am thy God: I will strengthen thee . . . I will help thee" . . . . Isaiah 41:10a. Sometimes in my shame and insecurities I want to hide from God. It is when I hide my face from Him that He finds me and welcomes me back into His arms. I feel blessed and assured that the promises of the Lord rests upon me. I know I have divine favor of the Lord over me, because of all the blessings He has willed to me. As I continue to believe the Lord for my salvation, and put my trust fully in Him, I utter these powerful words, Lord prepare me to be a sanctuary; Pure and holy; tried and true. Lord Jesus according to your word you have instructed me to be a holy sanctuary unto you, you have instructed me to present myself a living sacrifice unto you, holy and acceptable which is my reasonable service. Romans 12:1. *I beseech you therefore, brethren, by the mercies of God, that ye present your body a living sacrifice, holy, and acceptable unto God, which is your reasonable service*". This is my desire, O Lord to walk perfect before you. I want my heart to be your home. I want your home to be my sanctuary. I want to stay at your feet and learn of you. Lord Jesus, it is my desire to one day, live with you in heaven. You have stretched out your nail-print hands to me and said *"Don't let your heart be troubled. Trust in God, and trust also in me. There is more than enough room in my Father's home. If this were not so, would I have told you that I am going to prepare a place for you? When everything is ready, I will come and get you, so that you will always be with me where I am. And you know the way to where I am going."* *[John 14: 1 NLT]* . . . . " *"because I am the Way"* . . . John 14:6a

I remember the dream quite vividly, so many decades ago, of the outstretched arms of God calling me to Him. He has called me for a purpose. His opened arms were calling me to ministry. He was saying, "Today if you hear my voice, harden not your heart". Hebrews 3:8. "I will brand the call upon your memory, so that you will never forget it". He was saying, "I called you because you are mine and I will never leave you, neither will I forsake you". He was saying, I will shelter and protect you and uphold you with the right hand of my righteousness, because you will be in preparation for the Master's use.

And so it was that as I made a diligent search for my "Divine Call", the Spirit led me to the scripture according to Ephesians 4:1. The Apostle Paul said "*I therefore, the prisoner of the Lord, beseech you to walk worthy of the vocation [calling] wherewith ye are called*". I am called? Yes. I am called. Ha! I am humbled to know now that I am among the multitude of women that the Lord has called for His divine purpose.

The term "vocation" as Paul spoke of it, to the Ephesians people, is derived from the Latin word vōcātiō which is a "calling" from vōcāre, to call. What an amazing grace. But what is my vocation, what is my calling; and what is my occupation as it relates to the church. The scripture is full of passages that describes how we have been called to faith, how God calls us to a particular office or a particular way of life, for example, 2 Thessalonians 2: 14 said, "Whatever it is that we are called into, we are told to "walk worthy" of it. I know now as a Pastor's wife it was the Lord's doing to nurture me for this position. I know now as an Evangelist, it was the Lord's doing to cultivate me and infuse me with His Holy Spirit. I know now as a Bible teacher, it was the Lord who energized me and deposited knowledge in me to impart the Word to His people. I know now as a church organist, that the Lord has placed a song deep within me, so that as I play on the high sounding instruments, (Psalm 150) others would worship the Lord in spirit and in truth, and in the beauty of holiness. What an amazing grace. I pray each day for the Lord to bless me continually and use me through my creativity, my ideas, so that even the smallest task may bring Him glory and honor. Now I know what my purpose is, and with the help of God, will walk worthy of my vocation. The Bible according to Romans 11:29 in part said " . . . for the gifts and calling of God are irrevocable". It is unchangeable. Once you are called, you will always feel the urgency to respond. So then, what is a calling? Can anyone get one? My friend Bryant Wright who writes devotions and hosts the internet website by the name of "Right From The Heart", could not have summed it up any better. He said, and I quote "People struggle to understand what a calling is because it sounds so mystical and mysterious. A calling is an invitation or summons to leave what we're doing to serve someone who needs us. It always involves feelings of inadequacy because it moves us out of our comfort zone. It always involves sacrifice, unselfishness, and commitment for us to use our talents, abilities, and life experiences to serve God and man. A calling of God is always an inner leading from Him that is consistent with God's Word in Scripture. Can anybody be called? Everybody is. For the highest calling in life is not to be a teacher or public servant, not to be a pastor or a doctor, but to be a Christian and follow Jesus in faith. It's a calling for life and for eternity that you don't want to miss.

Have you accepted life's highest calling? ("Right From The Heart Daily Devotions/rightfromtheheart.org.")(with permission)

I praise the Lord once again for His hands on my life, because it is His divine favor and a gift sent special delivery from the throne of grace. So many times I have been approached by Men and Women of God, who has repeatedly confirmed my calling. One Bishop said to me during a revival service, "Woman of God, remember your dream. Go back and remember your dream." An apostle said to me, that the Lord had called me to be a prophetess, and I must obey the voice of the Lord." Another said to me that the Lord had called me into evangelism because my charisma is that of an evangelist. One said to me you will write that book. I thank God, because He has shown others that His spirit dwells within me. I thank God, because in each of those confirmations, the Lord had already shown me the vocation.

CHAPTER THREE

Praise And Worship

"Praise the LORD with the harp; make music to him on the ten-stringed lyre. Sing to him a new song; play skillfully, and shout for joy."—Psalm 33:2-3

Startled at the stillness of the congregation, because we have completed the congregational hymn of worship, I heard the moderator said from the pulpit, "This is the day that the Lord has made, let us rejoice and be glad in it." Psalm 118:24. O Lord you are our God and we will Praise You. You are our God and we will exalt you. Psalm 118:28. O give thanks to the Lord for He is good, for His mercy endures forever. Psalm 118:29. The ambiance is soaring now because praise and worship had already begun. The sound of music is the love of my soul. The Spirit of the Lord is truly in the place. Worship time is a blessing to me. All I can hear myself uttering is . . . . "God is Good" . . . . Gracious is the Lord . . . . God is merciful" Psalm 116:5 O Give thanks unto the Lord for He is good . . . . Psalm 118:1 Praise and worship time is a time when I personally reflect.

At that time every person, men, women, young people, elderly people, already standing from the recent procession, prepared themselves in anticipation for a grand old time in singing, clapping, skipping, shouting and dancing, some with tambourines in hand, especially a 92 year elderly woman. The music minister led everyone in singing "Hallelujah Praise the Lamb." Hallelujah Praise The Lamb." My Heart Sings His Praise Again, Hallelujah, Praise The Lamb." With outstretched hands pointed to the ceiling representing heaven, they sang "For He Alone Is Worthy, To Receive Our Praise and Glory". Lift Him Higher, In One Accord; Lift Our Praises To The Lamb".

"Excuse me". Excuse me daaling". "Praise da Lord". I heard someone said as the usher led another minister's wife to the Second Row where I was standing. Sereta apologized for being late as usual. "Traffic you know", she continued to get my attention. Very politely I hugged her and nodded to assure her that she is here now, that she had made it safely. "Glad you could make it". I said. "So how you doing, Sereta said to me while trying to settle and position her many bags on the floor beside us. By now everyone standing around our pew had their eyes focused on us. Quietly, I whispered so that no one could hear me. "I am blessed". You know, people who are late coming to church, always try to be a distraction to those around them. It's as though they try to bring attention to themselves. They always have many excuses, trying to raise a conversation about absolutely nothing, and I believe that one of the weapons the devil use to interrupt true worship is the action of habitual late comers. They come in noisily to get everyone's attention. Even though they come to church, they have not reached the place where there is a definite understanding of what praises to God is. They are late already, but they continue to rig up a conversation, about nothing. I believe in the presence of the Lord there must be total reverence.

Praise and worship at church is very important. In fact it is a very serious time for me personally. *Wikipedia Online Encyclopedia* defines *"Praise"* so beautifully in that it can be so understood by everyone. "In religion . . . . *it cites . . .* **praise** *is an impassioned exaltation of God, (ie. a Supreme Being, or Creation), typically as an expression of gratitude for one's life or being. Praise is an integral part of many religions, for example Christianity* *and Islam, which hold that God is a supreme being who is worthy of praise. The Biblical Book of Psalms is a collection of hymns and poems, many of which praise Yahweh. In Christianity, the word takes on a new meaning, and is understood as a command to either describe God or give a testimony of what God has done". (End quote)*

Everyone have their own personal preference for styles of worship music. Our church it seems is just not able to please everyone. We are a special blend of people from the Caribbean American culture. Most come seeking something. Some even come to be entertained. Our pastor consistently repeats that we are not a smorgasbord type ministry. Most that have come leave again and said our ministry is not quite what they were looking for. The church they said which they previously attended did it this way or that way. But if you look at it there are so many varieties of worship music styles. Some people like the band style of music, some just like the guitar and drums. Many people only enjoy songs and old hymns written before the 1900's while other people simply love the beauty of sweet organ music (which I play). Others especially the more youthful congregants are captivated by music with a pounding bass beat. In our church, most of the people love the contemporary music with a twist of the Caribbean influence. But at the end of the day praise and worship to me in essence is not about us and what we like. It is Praising God for what He has done for us and worshipping Him for who He is. It is simply gearing our reverence towards God our Father. As long as the music is centered on Christ and is grounded in the Word, then the variety of music, simply provide a method to glorify God and to allow more people to passionately worship Him. This is where we must embrace a deeper understanding of true worship. The Bible reminds us that those who worship knows not what they worship (John 4: 22a) But those that worship God must worship Him in spirit and in truth. John 4:24.

Well I thought, if I knelt again, Sereta would get the message. *James 4:7* said "Submit yourselves therefore to God. Resist the devil, and he will flee from you". Sometimes the devil comes in subtle ways like the person he uses to distract you from worshipping God. I believe every Christian must discern when the devil is in their midst. And so I knelt down in prayer again, and asked God to let me hide myself in Him . . . . "I have set the Lord always before me: Because He is at my right hand, I shall not be moved . . . ." Psalm 16:8. You know what, the devil fled. Sereta got the message, I think, because I could hear her voice beside me singing as well. I thought of many things right there down on my knees. I thought of the last communion service we had.

The Lord brought back to my recollection the recent Communion Ceremony. As I knelt at my seat, the first seat in the Second Row, I reflected on what the Lord had done for me, how He gave His precious life for me. I asked myself, what am I doing for the Lord. How am I building up His Kingdom? What am I giving Him in return that is precious too. I contemplated over my life and asked the Lord to forgive me of my sins. I have many transgressions. My righteousness is like filthy rags in Gods' sight, so I must ask Him again to cleanse me. I have many shortcomings, and insecurities, so I asked the Lord to take them away. I asked Him to take away the pain and the hurt and shame that I have experienced and endured. If we confess our sins, He said He is faithful and just and will forgive us our sins and purify us from all unrighteousness."—1 John 1:9. Then immediately, He brought me back to the answer He gave to Paul when Paul asked God to remove his thorns. God reminded me that His grace is sufficient for me. He said it to the Apostle Paul then, and He is saying the same thing to me today. "My grace is sufficient for you." 2nd Corinthians 12:9. So, before I partake of "the bread", His Body, and "the wine", His Blood, I thanked the Lord for giving me this humble privilege to partake at His table. O yes, He prepared a table before me in the presence of my enemies.

Then the song came back to me which brought drops of tears to my eyes. Not tears of sorrow, but tears of happiness, because I love the Lord. O how I love to be in communion with Him. I love to dwell in His presence. The lyrics of one particular song as I so recalled helped in reminding me always of who God is, His matchless awesomeness and the mighty power of His forgiveness. So it behooves me then, that all I can do for Christ is to present myself as a holy sacrifice to Him. The lyrics of that song and the psalm which it is written from are one which I recommend to all Christians today. Psalm 139:23-24 say, *"Search me, O God, and know my heart; try me and know my thoughts; and see if there is any wicked way in me, and lead me in the everlasting way."*

I once received an e-mail sent to me from a-Bible.com, an on-line daily devotion. As I read it I thought how wonderful the words are from the writer Fred G. Gibbs. These are the same thoughts I had about Psalm 139: 23-24, only he put it in a clearer perspective. His commentary read, and I must quote . . . . *"These are perhaps some of the most emotional words in the entire Bible. In these two verses there is so much. We see David asking God to search him, to look to the deepest part of what he is, his own heart. Why would David ask this? And, why would any of us ask it? The reason is simple. We cannot know our own hearts as well as God can. He indwells us, knows our every thought; He is aware of every feeling, and He understands us better that we do. If we ever needed anyone to reach down in the depths of our hearts to find out what is unholy so that it can be removed, it is God. Psalm 19:13 (NIV) said, "Keep back thy servant also from presumptuous sins; let them not have dominion over me; then shall I be upright, and I shall be innocent from the great transgression. Only God knows the heart. Man looks on the outside. Spiritual blindness and a carnal mind cannot see what God sees. Man sees only the outside"* (aBible.com)

I am often judged in a way contrary to what some of the people attending worship in our home church perceive a Christian should look like. I have been judged for a long period of time based upon the way I look on the outside. Whether it's my choice of hairstyle, or jewelry, or clothing, or even shoes, comments have been made from "Her heels are just too high" to "why does she paint her nails, are they real", or how about " . . .is her hair real". I am even resented because of the color of my skin. I have had to defend God many times by saying, "Hey, I was born that way". Being a Pastors wife for almost 20 years I have endured a volume of criticisms. But I believe it's not about my appearance, but about what my heart gives out. I have so much love in my heart to give. When I give it, it's so not appreciated. The story has been told that many do not understand me because I choose the sophisticated side of life. Nevertheless the Scripture reminds me that Jesus came unto His own, but His own people did not receive or welcome Him. Do you know that you can give ninety nine percent of yourself doing good for others and it goes un-noticed? But, one percent error is made out to be a mountain peak of misdeeds. It happens to us every-day. It's the unappreciative and ungrateful nature of humans. Remember the story of the ten lepers, only one went back to thank Jesus.

On the matter of my choice of clothing and accessories I allow the Lord to lead and guide me and I believe they are very tasteful choices. I believe the Lord is pleased at my preference of clothing. I dress for Him, because He is my bridegroom. I dress for Him on the inside and on the outside as well. I love the way the Holy Spirit tells me when He is not pleased with what I choose to wear for that day. He would nudge me to change, and I select something else with a little laughter in the end. But on the secular side I have been in Public Administration for almost 28 years. As a Senior Paralegal dealing with corporate and civil law for the town government I have had to deal with many officials from State level to local and judicial level. Representing my company in a professional manner is expected. I bring the Lord with me to work, and I am respected because of the way I carry myself as a Christian. Many times I am asked to give the invocation before a town-hall meeting. When grief visits the workplace, I am called upon to offer comfort. In our church, I endeavor to be an example for all the ladies, young and old, saved and unsaved. I have seen some of the young ladies try to conduct themselves like I do, in their standing, sitting with a straight posture with hands folded on lap, praying style, and even attempting to use handkerchiefs on their knees while sitting. As a matter of fact, many of the ladies, some even older have taken up the style of using coordinating handkerchiefs at church. I use hankies for a special reason and it's biblical from the book of Acts. So I don't know why I am held in contempt by some. Actually, women have left the ministry, because they said I am nothing more than a phony and they cannot worship under the same roof with me. I think that's judging another. A Passage from John 7:24(a) said, "Do not judge by appearances, but judge with right judgment." I read an article which said "a recent survey was taken which shown that some women have a tendency to be resentful of pastors wives". Pastors' wives, many of whom are humble people by virtue of the office they hold are not to be held in low estate but in high regard. To the husband who does not recognize the wife out of fear of losing members, the Bible according to 1 Peter 3:7 (ESV) said, "Likewise, husbands, live with your wife in an understanding way, showing honor to the woman as the weaker vessel, since they are heirs with you of the grace of life, so that your prayers may not be hindered." Husbands, preachers, be forewarned. Many husbands, preachers and pastors are out there having their prayers hindered because they fail to honor their wife. Let us not be carried away in ignorance, but rather walk in the truth. Respect must be given to the wife by the husband first so that the congregation will see it, recognize it and follow suit. Bible said "My people perish because of lack of knowledge. Hosea 4:6 KJV. I can understand if one was not taught to do the right thing, but every pastor must have a teachable spirit to know what is right from that which is wrong.

To me I feel that pastors wives are Gods fine and delicate china that must be carefully handled. If not handled carefully we will be broken into many pieces physically, emotionally, and unfortunately, psychologically. But God and God only, should be the one to break us, not man. God as the Ultimate Potter, He is the only one capable of putting us back together again in the way only He wants to mold us. Also, it is important to know that we are the Pastors "neck", "backbone" and "spine". If Pastors wives are broken, the Pastor will fall short. If we are abused by the congregation, the Pastor is ultimately affected in his ministering. If he is affected, his work is bothered so much so that he cannot hear from God or see clearly the tasks that God has assigned him to do. So that is why his neck is so important. I can't see a head without a neck. And so, this is why I continue to conduct myself in a way that is pleasing to God. The Bible said, "Judge not, lest you be judged". So why would one resort to disdain another to scorn and take Holy Communion at the same time. Why would we raise from our knees in prayer, but gossip about another. We must be ever so careful. If we spend too much time criticizing, we have no time to love. Anyone who thinks of himself more highly than another because he say to himself "I am the epitome of what God expect others to be" . . . , is simply a person walking in pride and is therefore a liar.

When a woman thinks or measures herself solely by her exterior qualities, she sets herself up to be faulted. She appears shallow and narrow-minded to others, and thus is only fooling herself. She is not walking in the Grace of God. Such a one may fool others but does not fool God. On the other hand, when a woman wears her gift of grace, elegance and love from the heart, the hidden elegance portrays Gods love on the outside. One doesn't have to tell because it's written all over, in the manner of her speech, and her godly actions, she portrays the love of Christ. It's like something on the inside, working on the outside. We call that the Holy Spirit at work. Wearing a hat on one's head, or refraining from wearing any exterior enhancements such as cosmetics is only a fraction of what it takes to be a Christian. Refraining from wearing soft delicate jewelry to compliment one's femininity, or wearing hideous clothing to give a picture of submissiveness, is probably also only a fraction of what it takes to be a Christian. In fact, this does not constitute being a Christian at all. It is simply only the personal choice that such an individual embraces. It is a made up rule imposed upon the congregation by their leader. Notwithstanding, it is within the chambers of our heart that it matters most. Remember, God is looking for true worshippers. He is not looking for a man or a woman based upon what the appearance is from the outside. Humans look only on the outside, but God, Hallelujah! He looks on the inside. We are to rend our hearts and not our garments. Our Pastor always said to us, "You don't have to wear a frown on your face to give the outward show of being a child of God". You don't have to wear a lapel either which reads "Christian", for others to see. Children of the Most High must look good, and behave themselves, and one of the places it's exhibited is in ones beautiful smile, and the love of God they represent.

So the next time before we take Holy Communion, let us consider the hurts we have inflicted on others by a selfish gesture or even by just a malicious remark. Sometimes we hold others in contempt and disdain without even knowing why. Pride and Communion do not go hand in hand. Just in case we do not understand fully what pride is, it is an excessively high opinion of oneself. Actuality, it is one of the six sins that God hates according to Proverbs 6:15-16; and as a matter of fact it is placed first on the list above a liar. It was pride which caused Lucifer to be cast out of heaven.

Additionally, pride is defined as "undue confidence in and attention to one's own skills, accomplishments, state, possessions, or position. Many biblical words describe this concept, each with its own emphasis. Some of the synonyms for pride include arrogance, presumption, conceit, self-satisfaction, boasting, and high-mindedness. It is the opposite of humility, the proper attitude one should have in relation to God. Pride is rebellion

against God because it attributes to self the honor and glory due to God
alone. Proud people do not think it necessary to ask forgiveness of others
because they do not admit their sinful condition. This attitude toward God
finds expression in one's own attitude toward others, often causing people
to have a low estimate of the ability and worth of others and therefore to
treat them with either contempt or cruelty. Some have considered pride
to be the root and essence of sin. Others consider it to be sin in its final
form. It is an inordinate self-esteem; an unreasonable conceit of one's own
superiority in talents, beauty, wealth, accomplishments, rank or elevation
in office, which manifests itself in lofty airs, distance, reserve, and often in
contempt of others. [*KJV On-line Bible Dictionary*].

   Having read this definition in its complete entirety, it is obvious that we
have all sinned and have come short of the glory of God. We are all guilty.
We judge others among and around us. We even judge people we don't know.
Sometimes we say nothing in effect, but don't you know that it is better to
confess it to God? Admitting our shortcomings is better in the long run
than continuing in it because it is only a clever and subtle type of sin. It's
the sin of judging others by their appearance. The last time I checked, God
is the painter, and we are the finished product. When He was finished, He
said, "That's good". Don't have the audacity to discredit God, by judging
others. Who are we to correct God? Whatever color he chose to paint us in
we must accept and admire it. Because we are Gods' finished picture. Listen,
on the next communion service, we had better pray for forgiveness on this
thing call pride before we partake of God's Body and His Precious Blood.
The Bible said if we do it unworthily, this is the greatest sin. Remember
what happened to Judas? He was there in the body at the Last Supper. But
his heart was corrupt. He had another motive. Let us not fool ourselves.
Communion is a beautiful and sacred observance. Jesus said, as often as we
do it we must do it in His remembrance.

Praise and Worship was winding up and the last song meant to be a personal testimony for everyone, brought much tears to my eyes. The lyrics are so like what I prayed for.

"Draw Me Close To You
Never Let Me Go
You Laid It All Down Again
Just To Say That You're My Friend
Help Me Find The Way
Bring Me Back To You"

"Mother"! "I am praying for you Mother", I heard someone said, as she came by my side and wrapped her arms around me, from where I knelt. I stood to my feet, and we just stood there and hugged. By now many had already thronged the altar to surrender to the Holy Spirit. There is no greater form of worship than full surrendering of self to the Spirit. This is where you shut everything and everybody out. And your focus is solely on Jesus, the One who has redeemed you.

There were those standing there in need of prayer for various requests. The Spirit brought to my heart the story of a man with leprosy as the Bible has taught us from Luke Chapter Five. The Bible said "*₁₂And it came to pass, when He [Jesus]was in a certain city, behold a man full of leprosy: who seeing Jesus fell on his face, and besought him, saying, Lord, if thou wilt, thou canst make me clean. ¹³And he put forth his hand, and touched him, saying, I will: be thou clean. And immediately the leprosy departed from him. ¹⁴And he charged him to tell no man: but go, and shew thyself to the priest, and offer for thy cleansing, according as Moses commanded, for a testimony unto them.[Luke 5: 12-14KJV]*

What new revelation was the Spirit communicating? Is it that we are all so filled with all kinds of corruption? Well yes. We are all spiritual lepers.

And until we come to the place and fully surrender to Christ, we cannot be made clean. We have to take off the stuff; the "stuff" that so easily beset us. Hebrews 12:1 said "Wherefore seeing we also are compassed about with so great a cloud of witnesses, let us lay aside every weight, and the sin which doth so easily beset us, and let us run with patience the race that is set before us". Every now and then we have all kinds of stuff that hangs on and latches itself to us. We have guilt and embarrassment, disappointments and disgraces, that we feel so shameful at times. How about malice, envy and jealousy? How about greed and cheating? How about being cruel to one another? How about being mean and nasty? O yes we are spiritual lepers. We need a wash. What can wash away our sins? The response came back to me, "nothing but the blood of Jesus."

I see the Pastor proceeding from his overseers chair to the pulpit and from there he begins to pray for and over the congregation. Sometimes, he would descend from the pulpit to the lower altar, and from there he anoints them with oil and laid his hands upon them. He prays for the sick, who comes to church for healing, he prays for financial blessings for those who are going through the storms of life economically; he prays for the depressed, discouraged, lonely and abused. He prays for marriages, relationships, physical health, emotional health, and broken homes. One prayer in particular that I hear the pastor pray, is the prayer for disobedient children, runaways, and mean supervisors, who are constantly at war with God's people. These supervisors seems to be the devils co-horts in that they refuse to let up and offer Sundays off when requested, so that Gods people can go to church. Instead, they would offer Sundays off to unbelievers I am told by many in our church who are affected by this malicious deed. They are even on the attack I am told for Wednesday Bible Studies as well. There are some major employers in Florida, who are guilty of this scheme. In fact this demonized spirit could well be deposited in mean supervisors who these companies hire not just in Florida but all over the world. Remember the

Bible tells us that "the devil comes to kill, steal and to destroy". What harm does it take to give a little? I believe none at all. A contented employee is an efficient employee. An efficient employee is a productive employee, thus rendering a better service to their employer who gains in the long run.

Prayers being completed, much tears being shed, and many relieved of their burdens, went back to their seat while the Pastor ascends back to his overseers chair and his ministers and altar attendants proceed to theirs. "The joy of the Lord is my strength" I thought. He is the source of my strength and the strength of my life.

"C'mon somebody, let's praise the Lord". "Hallelujah"! The moderator continued, "Let us stay in His presence with thanksgiving". "Let us give him praise until something happens. "Thank you Jesus."

CHAPTER FOUR

My First Missionary Journey

"But when He, the Spirit of truth, comes, He will guide you into all truth. He will not speak on his own; He will speak only what He hears, and He will tell you what is yet to come."—John 16:13

The Pastor announced from the pulpit after his sermon on Mothers' Day, that he would like to see the following people in his office after the fellowship today. Well one of the names mentioned was mine. I was startled and anxious, because being seated in the second row; most times I am never recognized or even acknowledged as Pastors wife. I feel invisible on many occasions, so I resort to much meditation as I stay seated. I was told by an old mother that a pastor's wife must be a quiet spirited person. I ponder over many things there, and deliberate about them in my heart so as to feel better and also to allow the spirit to move within me. There has always been an inner struggle about this issue of non-recognition, so I was surprised that the Pastor even mentioned my name. Sometimes I feel that I am a stranger at the church and not the Pastors wife. It is not unusual for people to address the Pastor even on special occasions without recognizing me as First Lady as well. So used to being overlooked, I was very surprised when Pastor mentioned my name.

As we approached his office, after the mother's day fellowship luncheon was ended, we each walked sheepishly down the corridor wondering what we had done wrong. Normally when we get called to pastors office as a group, sometimes, it's not so much of good news, but then at other times, it's for obtaining future assignments. Still at other times it's for a reprimand too. Pastor was already seated at his desk as we each approached and he asked us to be seated. He told us to "Relax" "it's not bad news". I don't know about the others but I felt a sigh of relief, when he told us we were each chosen to go on a missionary trip. We thought it was a journey into another city like Orlando, Miami, or another nearby town. We were so not thinking internationally.

The air was silent for a moment. Each of us discovered that we were going to Jamaica and we were scheduled to be leaving on August 18. My heart sank, because I did not know what to expect. Then Pastor said bluntly, " . . . and you cannot say no". We laughed nervously, because we knew that after all the years in ministry missions trip was a prerequisite to having a title as a missionary or evangelist. We just didn't know when we would have the opportunity to go. After we were interviewed by Pastor, it turned out that I was the only one who had not yet traveled on missions. As nervous as I was, the Lord brought me back to a dream that I previously had of me being in a far country. In the dream, I was fully dressed in red clothing, and standing on a stage ministering to a very enormous crowd. In the congregation were the other two missionaries who are now in assignment with me. It's amazing how God shows you things to come when you stay in His presence.

On Saturday August 18, a bright and sunny day in Florida, a delegation consisting of myself another evangelist and her son, and a missionary who is a nurse, boarded an aircraft heading to Jamaica for a convention. This would be my first missionary journey, but not the first for the others. The most significant thing about this trip was that we were headed directly in the eye of one of the most devastating hurricanes ever. "DEAN" was its name, a monster some called it. Dean was a category 5 hurricane. Because I knew we would eventually get a direct hit I had to put my total trust in the Lord for deliverance and a way of escape.

I believed that the Lord would take us through the storm and keep us safe. I had to trust him so much more now than ever, so I trusted Him and put my life in His hands. I had no doubt then that everything would be alright. We said our good byes to the pastor who had driven us to the airport. Once in the air, we settled in our seats and my work as a prayer warrior began. I began to pray. I prayed and thanked the Lord for safety. I put the aircraft in the hands of the Lord. I prayed for almost the entire duration of the flight because the next sound I heard was the pilot telling us that we should prepare for landing. We landed safely in Montego Bay. Where did all the time went. It had to have been God. He piloted the plane. Lord I thank you. There was absolutely and positively no turbulence. How could this be unless God was aboard? The Bible reminded me that "the effectual fervent prayer of a righteous man availeth much. James 5:17. Upon landing in Montego Bay, on schedule, during a massive hurricane warning we were told we would need to change planes to a bigger aircraft. Reason, the last plane that was on the island would transport us to Kingston because all aircrafts are returning to Florida or other parts of the U.S.A for safety.

However, other aircrafts were landing to let people on to our aircraft in route to the US.A. as well. This whole operation took about five hours. During those horrific five hours, we had no communication. No one offered food or water or any information whatsoever. We stood in a very hot corridor in the airport. Someone said air conditioning was restricted to certain areas, one of which was not the corridor where we stood. We were located at gate # 6. We stayed there from 2:50 pm until 6:35pm, when we finally boarded the plane again. After that, we again sat in an air conditioned aircraft from 6:45pm until about 8:00 pm. Our trip from Montego Bay to Kingston would take only 40 minutes. On board, the passengers became very agitated and some showed signs of agitation. One passenger expressed her displeasure and deep resentment against the airline industry. She stated that she has been waiting since 2:00pm that same day, for a 40 minute trip. Another passenger who stated that she was a kidney patient took a stand and began to calm down the angry passengers. She was verbally attacked with profanity.

During that time of uncertainty, I prayed like I never prayed before I sang in my spirit like I never sang before. Finally we were told that the delay was due to the fact that our aircraft was arranging for all stranded passengers on another island since there were many available seats on ours. The airline I was on was the last aircraft remaining on the island. I did not understand why we were not told this information before. The aircraft finally came in filled with disabled military young men and women who all had prosthetic limbs of some sort. Anyhow, I look at this challenge as a great act of humanitarianism. My waiting was not in vain. I thought, how could anyone allow our U.S. disabled soldiers and marines to be stranded on an island during a storm. The Lord was in control. After landing safely in Kingston, we located our luggage and headed for the exit. Now the handler for the ministry-mission would be there waiting for us. So I assumed; because neither of us knew each other. Our delegation didn't know them, and they did not know us. Had we not been delayed everything would have gone smoothly and on schedule. But it was very late and everyone had already gone home. But God intervened. A woman standing bashfully to the side of the loading docks made a visual eye contact with me. Instantly I held visual contact with her as well. She boldly approached me to inquire of me if I was First Lady, Evangelist Brown, and with a smile of relief, I answered YES! And with a question of my own, I too inquired, "Are you by chance Evangelist Samuels". Immediately, with much sigh of relief, we smiled like we have known each other for many years, hugged me and we made our way to introduce the others.

After all our bags and luggage were loaded securely on the missions transport, we settled ourselves in the vehicle but before we pulled away from the airport we went into a prayer of thanksgiving to the Lord for we were now safe and among Gods' people. Contact was made with our leader Bishop Wilson. I spoke with him on the cell phone, and he too was relieved as well. They had waited for us almost all day with absolutely no means of communication. They had phoned the airport and were told that we were not on board. But what the airline industry failed to disclose to them is that we were all waiting at Gate #6 for further transport to Kingston, the final part of our trip. Although there was no communication, God would prevail.

We travelled about another hour or more through what seemed to be a ghost town. Everywhere was closed down and boarded up. No humans on the streets other than a few vehicles hastily making their way to safety. The island was in eminent and severe danger. Hurricane Dean was a Category 5 status, heading to make a direct hit on Jamaica. It appeared from what I have been observing—which it was—that everyone was leaving Jamaica. I mean the tourists and visitors—but we are heading into Jamaica. Faith is what we are taught. Faith is what we use to condition ourselves as God's chosen believers. We are taught to follow the example of the Apostle Paul as he endured the circumstances surrounding his missionary journeys. In one particular instance the bible said he was ship-wrecked. The Bible also said no lives were lost. So we had no fright or panic among us because we had already left everything into Gods hands.

We arrived safely at the mission at after midnight on the 19th of August. The place was quiet. The staff, those who lived there, were either already in bed and others were gone home. We were ushered down a dim hallway to a small room which was already occupied with 2 beds inside. An elderly woman was asleep in one of the beds. Five of us would now have to share the same little room consisting of the two small beds a dresser and a closet. There were us three adult missionaries, the elderly woman who told us she was born in 1928, and a five year old child. As Christians, we united and what a beautiful rest that was. I awoke about 5:00a.m. Sunrise was welcoming. I found a bathroom down the same hallway which had a shower. It was very humbling accommodations which remind me that one of the fundamentals of being Christ-like is humility. I took a shower and as the very cold water touched my body, I sang to the Lord to get the frigid shock of cold water off my mind. Not knowing that this would be my last wash for days to come, I casually exited the bathroom for others to accommodate themselves.

As the morning came I could hear people praying in the sanctuary across from the living facility. About this facility, I came to realize that it is more like a church hotel so to speak that house about 250 people to sleep. Some rooms had from six to at least eight beds. They would sleep at least two to a bed. There was a cafeteria which provide for at least four hundred people per schedule daily. In the U.S.A. this is a facility would be designated a hurricane shelter based upon the structural advantages. About 8:30 a.m. we were called to a rich breakfast. What a banquet. Fried breadfruit, Ackee and codfish, plantains, calalloo, which is a native green vegetable from the spinach family, bakes, which is like a hot biscuit, fresh tropical fruits, cooked ground provisions, juices, and so many other things which dressed the table. One would wonder why such a hearty meal in the morning. Well this diet is the reason why so many of the natives live so long past 100 years old. After such a meal one is expected to work all day long, and then have a similar evening meal. However, as we ate of the delicious meal, we did not hesitate to take pleasure becoming acquainted with other delegates. After the rich and hearty breakfast was completed, we went back to our rooms and got dressed for Sunday Convention. I well remembered a dream I previously had. In the dream, I saw myself in a theater ministering to an auditorium of people, too many to be counted. I always remembered that dream, and shuffled the pages of my memory as to what it meant. Only, I did not know that the dream would unravel on the day that I was getting dress for Sunday Convention. I had packed a beautiful red dress in my luggage. My wardrobe for the day was a chiffon red dress, a red hat and other coordinating accessories like my lap kerchief. It was the same dress I saw in the dream. After we all were fully clothed we made our way downstairs to the place of worship.

The outer-bands of the hurricane had made its approached very slowly but no one even considered the consequences. We went into church and what an edifice. It was a great cathedral with pews to hold about 800 people seated and a facility to accommodate 1500 with tents and portable seats, so I was told. As the minister led the consecration service, the Lord sent someone "an usher" by the direction of the Bishop to escort us to the pulpit. To me this was a great honor. The power of the Lord moved in the place all day. One only had to be there to experience the joyfulness of His anointing. Without any thought of it I looked at my wrist watch. Hurricane Dean was beginning to show his wrath and I was becoming a concerned. It was now 2:00p.m. The winds were furious by now but no one seemed to take notice. The feast was prepared and hosted by the bishop's wife. Although the tables were spread admirably, with all the banquet trimmings that you could feast upon, I could only but focus on the blustery weather outside. The winds were intense. After dinner, the radio broadcasted that all electrical power would be shut off at 5:00pm. Because water utilities were controlled by power, water would be shut off as well.

The forceful band of rain was upon us now at approximately 5:03pm, Sunday August 19. It was torrentuous. It was fierce. It was angry. I looked at it as it howled an angry sound of discontent. Electricity was eventually shut off and the indoor plumbing water stopped its flow. I watched from the window of my little room as the roof of the cathedral began to rip from its beams. I saw a deep hole gashed in the corrugated zinc roof and the cedar beams snapped like match sticks. Dean was on a massive rampage to destroy whatever was in its path. We held hands and began to pray again.

One of our missionaries had a battery powered lantern. Thank God this helped us because there was no light in the place. Night came quickly and the place was dark, humid and hot. But we continued to look outside at the wrath of hurricane Dean. All I could hear were the frightened cries of people down the several hallways. We continued to pray and this would be the beginning of a fourteen hour ordeal because Dean lingered over us for the entire night.

Mostly everyone slept in their Sunday clothes or other sorts of clothing that night. I had already changed earlier into a caftan so I was feeling more comfortable. During the night, the rain spewed its torrents upon us inside our rooms. The windows had no protective covering over them so we made several attempts to seal the slats with old newspaper or towels. The smell of the storm was rancid. It smelt like sulfur and salt.

It was horrid and noisy. The sound was like the crashes of ten trains colliding. Squeal and howling seemed to be the norm. The howl of tree trunks ripping from concrete and street pavements was the usual sound for hours to come. It's as though you could hear the roads bursting like enormous water balloons. The wind was not letting go of its victims such as trees, and buildings and anything else in its way. Anything in Dean's path would have to show some respect or be battered down to the ground. He was fierce. To no avail we gave up trying to cover the window slats, and I decided to just as well go to sleep. I prayed to God for deliverance, repented of my sins, and put my life into the hands of the Lord. Fortunately, the Lord gave me sweet sleep. I was awakened several times in the night only briefly to realize that the monster Dean was still lurking outside. About 5:00 a.m. The next morning, I heard a group of people singing the song "*Draw me Nearer, Nearer, Nearer Blessed Lord—to thy precious bleeding side.*" Others joined in. I realized that it was Monday morning. We were saved. Gods' favor had rested upon us. He kept us safe in the eye of the storm until the storm had passed over us.

Monday morning, August 20, was a day I would never forget. There was no electricity at the mission but I could see dimly that some women still had their church hats on. Men also still wore their suits from the day before. Some had shirt and tie on with sleeves all rolled up. I heard the voice of the Bishop. People were sending up praises to God for how He had saved them all and that no one was hurt, neither were there any fatalities. I joined in the thanksgiving worship as well. God had saved us one more time, and it was another day the Lord had kept us. Monday morning, the day after the aftermath I looked out my window and I saw God's bright sunshine. Preparation for restoring the building was underway already by the bishop who led the undertakings. We all helped in way that was necessary. No one spoke. We just helped in every possible area that we could. People were clearing away debris. Tree branches and scattered fruits and other household items were strewn about the place. Power poles and trees were down. Some homes were torn apart and dismantled. The roofs of many although still in place, showed signs of being severely battered. The once lush and fertile trees bearing fruits in abundance were bent out of its current healthy shape to being stressed and battered; their bark stripped to its sap and eaten away. Leaves and branches were now being swept in piles to be burnt. As I too looked around the compound, I wondered what would have happened had it been worst. Yet in the total devastation, it was reported that there were no fatalities. I again thanked God for his tender mercies. He reminded me again, with a slight rebuke, "Have I not said, that I would never leave you neither would I forsake you".

I found a straw broom and began to sweep the muddy water from the hallway in the big auditorium. As I swept along with the others, a good feeling of delight and peace resonate over me because I was to be a part of the clean-up team. I glanced back earlier the same morning when everything was not visible. As the dawn lit my room I observed that my bed linen was covered with dirt and leaves. My clothes, bed linen and pillow and that of the other missionaries too, were soaked with storm water and leaves from the battered trees, and dirt as well. I didn't mind sleeping on the damp bed because it could have been worst. Scattered rugs were soaked, but we were all O.K., so I continued to sweep with tears in my eyes. My job was to relocate the chairs and tables that were strewn about, and all the displaced cups and bowls and mugs and bring everything in that assignment to some kind of normalcy. Then I mopped up water from around the place as best as I could. Missionary Eve was on the other side working as well. It seemed as though the cathedral was destroyed and the sheet rock all fell from the ceiling and was everywhere. The altar in the cathedral was destroyed, so she helped in cleaning up. When we finally met up, she had a lot of white soot and dust all over her face. We laughed, and someone mentioned that they would have loved to take a picture of "First Lady" and Missionary Eve looking this way. We laughed as well, saying Pastor would not believe it either.

Tree branches were everywhere. In fact, when I woke to make my bed there were leaves in my bed. I laughed because I had no idea what had happened to me during the night when the Lord put me to sleep. The Lord allowed a sleep to fall over me while he covered me under the shadows of his righteous hands. Scripture verses were on my mind as the storm raged on the outside. One of them was Isaiah 45. Then is when I fell asleep. But as I woke I realized that there was no electricity and no water either. We managed to accommodate ourselves in the best way we knew how. I don't believe the people at the mission facility had made preparation at all. Because there were no lamps, there was no generator or "stand-by" as they call it there. There were no containers filled with water. Comparably, in the U.S.A., a hurricane of this nature would call for hurricane preparedness to be underway including evacuations to higher grounds. The local and state government would be vigilant on this account. But accordingly, nothing seemed to have been in place. A standby is what is known as a generator in the U.S. There was none at the mission. For a crowd that size, there was no bottled water either.

Shortly, we were called to eat. After brunch, we prepared to go out on our first mission journey. We passed out tracks and offered words of hope and love of Jesus to those who just overwhelmingly in dismay stood by the roadside or by their destroyed houses. We finally arrived to a house where an elderly woman lived. The condition was extremely deplorable; the house was completely destroyed from the hurricane. There was no roof and whatever cardboard ceiling still existed was sopping with dirty muddy water. To release the pressure, we puckered holes in the cardboard ceiling to allow the muddy water to leak onto the floor below. The beds and old sofas were waterlogged and ultimately destroyed. Walls began to mold and mildew set in that fast because of the humidity. The tile floor was covered in muddy water. Nothing of her was spared. We could find nothing dry to clothe her in. She showed signs of trauma because all she continuously said is that "I was born in December 21, 1921; so figure it out because I don't know how old I am". Due to the trauma, we concluded that she was confused. She kept saying alternately in the Jamaican dialect, "See" "*E fill wi wata*". "*All unda de bed ha wata*". So as someone prepared a makeshift bath for her, I found an old mop and mopped the muddy water from underneath her bed. Don't you know she kept a machete there? I smiled and left it just as I found it. But I tried the best way to remove the water, carefully wringing its dirty liquid with my bare hands. I had no thought of diseases because God's hands were doing the work. I told her after she had her bath, that there was no more water under the bed. And was she happy. She laughed showing the broadest grin with her prominent un-brushed false teeth. Later on in a new house dress and new underwear, she felt better. She appeared coherent. We had packed and taken along with us, bags of clean clothing, and bars of bath soap just in case. A woman from the yard next door combed her tousled hair. After all this we said a prayer for her. We sang a hymn with her too. Before we said good bye, we encouraged her and told her we would return to check in on her before returned to the U.S.A.

On our trip around the hurricane ravaged villages, we spoke with several people and continued to give out tracks and offer hope to those who just stood by with nothing to do. Interestingly, no one seemed to care. No one was cleaning up. No one was trying to help themselves. People were just in a daze and were just standing about. Eventually we came to a store which had a tavern. We stopped by the tavern bar because we saw so many able-bodied men just sitting there around the tavern portico. They all appeared hopeless. We went over to greet them because apparently one of our missionaries recognized one of the men. One of the men saw my shoes before he even looked up at me. He begged me for them. I said to him sadly, "Sir, if I gave them to you what would I wear now, as you can see the place is graveled and muddy". He said, "But I like your shoes. You have pretty toes." I offered him a track and said, "This is something to read while you are waiting here and to also remember me and my pretty toes". He accepted the tracked and promised to read it. We took the journey back to the mission. In fact we had no idea how far we had all walked. Upon arriving back at the mission, we discovered there was still no electricity. The weather was so hot and humid. God had blessed us to have some drinking water which was closely rationed.

Water was getting very scarce. There wasn't much left to flush the toilets so we had to take our rationed bath water and poured it out afterwards into the toilets. We were told that when the power was cut off the water went as well. So washing ourselves properly was becoming difficult. I had one cup of water which was actually a beautiful treasure. On Tuesday, August 21, a water truck delivered water to the people at the mission. Anything that could hold water was used to catch the precious recourse. Buckets of all shape and sizes were used. Basins, pitchers, mugs, and anything that the helpers could find of which after they were filled was deposited into a large drum on the upstairs level for easy access later.

This commodity could be used for cooking, washing, bathing and flushing of the toilets for two days. But we could only flush the toilets with the wash or bath water. That was difficult. We prayed that no one would get sick from contamination or other diseases. Flies and mosquitoes were beginning to swarm the place. It was hot and miserable, and the stench from the toilets began to pervade the corridors. In order to keep healthy, lots of fruits were provided as another option for drinking water, in fact it was the best thing to ingest at the moment. I had oranges, and mangoes, custard apples, a creamy sweet artichoke like fruit, and home grown bananas as well, but apparently, too much variety is not good I soon learned.

Early the next day, I had an onset of a severe case of diarrhea. "Not now" I said. The diarrhea was not good. What a bad timing. I thought I was extremely careful. I used hand sanitizers every moment for everything. I was careful not to touch anything unclean. But apparently, I was contaminated in some way. But I believed God for my healing. Earlier that morning, my thought went back to the prayer meeting which was held in an upstairs cafeteria. Men, women and young people had all gathered there. Our delegation joined in as well. Two ministers were present this time around. We sang beautiful songs and prayed. Shortly afterwards I was asked to deliver the Word. It was an honor. The Lord led me to Isaiah 61. Sharing the Word was a refreshing experience. All the people were so into receiving the precious words. They were hungry for the Word. After all was done a healing miracle took place. One young man who had worked on the roof the day before had injured his back. He was in a lot of pain. During the prayer of deliverance, he rose from his seat, stood up, and began to glorify God. He gave praises to God for healing him. We clapped as our way of thanking God for the miracle as well. We then greeted everyone in Jesus name and in ending that early Morning Prayer meeting, breakfast was served, and we ate in the quiet darkness—shy of one lit candle which sat strategically in the center of a table. We thanked God for what we were about to receive and ate with joy and thanksgiving. My stomach was imploding. The pain was unbearable. I believe my neighbor sitting next to me could hear the grumbling sound of my belly. I knew it was a different kind of pain. It was the pain when one was about to have a severe stomach virus. It is happening. We were all going to be sick. Lord help me! I cried out silently. Sugar ants, flies and mosquitoes were already out from their hiding places. Still not good! The funny thing, these minor setbacks did not bother anyone but me. I smiled silently again.

If anyone could guess the temperature, it would be so not me. Somebody said it was 100_0. Hot and humid was the status quo. My energy level was already low. I remembered I had my blood pressure medicine in my luggage. I took one pill and lay down on my assigned bed. Yes I had the runny stomach by now which was not good, and there was no water to flush it away because no one had taken an afternoon bath. I was fearful, and one of the ministers came to my assistance, and comforted me. She said, "Don't worry—we understand. We will see about the toilet and sort things out". She made it happened. Water was brought up to flush the toilet. Thanks to God. I was feeling very sick by now. Another missionary from England was also sick. I didn't know the other people there so I couldn't give a count of who became ill. I continued to lie down in the bed which was a little dryer from the nights before. The bishop's wife gave me clean sheets, pillow cases, and towels as I was getting noticeably despondent in my countenance. No water, I so wanted to go home. But God delivered. Someone brought a bucket of water to me of which I was able to pour into it an antibacterial liquid called "Detol" and tried to wash my face and wipe myself down, being careful not to spill any of the precious liquid. It smelt like Lysol. The toothless old woman, said to me "*hav fe use Detol*". Detol is a disinfectant used to cleanse the water for public use. In America, after a water contamination we use similar products like chlorine to prevent diseases and contamination. Thank God for water and Detol. My friends washed themselves as well as the little boy who was with us. This little boy named "Dennis" was a five year old diabetic. We prayed that God would cover him under His blood so that he would not get sick on us.

So far God had done just that. While I sat on the bed looking out through the window, I saw Dennis playing and running about with the other little children. What a joy that was to look at. I so wanted to go outside again. The other ladies had gone out in the streets to witness. I made a decision to stop drinking whatever was placed before me to drink, for fear of ingesting a parasite and resorted to drinking hot bottled soda pops instead. Kola Champagne was good to swallow. So I rationed my bottles.

Wednesday, August 22, I rose very early about 6:15 a.m. in the morning. I could only imagine what the day would bring. Suddenly I heard roosters crowing and dogs barking. The place was very quiet, for everyone was still asleep. I recalled on the Monday before when the bishop decided to take us on a tour of the pig pens. I have never been in a pig pen before. Bishop explained that the pigs were raised on the premises to be consumed as meat for the citizens. The chickens were raised for eggs and food. One pig in particular weighed about 500 pounds. This was the largest pig I have ever seen. Maybe he weighed more but not less. The bishop referred to the pigs as "cow-hogs". So we had a lite breakfast of fried eggs, plantains, chicken sausages-Jamaican hard-o-bread, and of course, my favorite freshly peeled oranges picked from the trees that were not affected by the hurricane. There was still a water ration. No water was found anywhere, in spite of the heavy rains which fell during the hurricane. There was still no electricity. We ate in darkness, and slept in total darkness. I had another bout of diarrhea. This was very bad especially since there was no water to flush the toilet. The bathrooms began to smell very bad. One could only understand why. There was a preacher named Minister Anglin. She made things happened. She had everything sorted out, and attended to us very well. Evangelist Morris began to show signs of distress. She is a full figured woman. She was showing signs of severe fatigue, and possible heat exhaustion. She was always very hot, perspired a lot and her energy level was getting extremely low. However, we found the time to quickly dress to leave for our missionary duties.

Two days before, and that would be Monday afternoon, we had a discussion with a young girl who thought that telling us a short story was just another story. The story was told like this:

"You waa me tell yu a stoary 'bout a bline hooman"? Well . . . . she began in her dialect, which I understood quite well and interpret for the purpose of this book, There is an old lady who lives on my street. She is blind. She is being beaten by bad boys and girls who took over her house and throws her outside to live in the outdoor toilet". This caught our immediate attention. She continued her story. "Sometimes they beat her with sticks and poke brushwood at her and beat her. It is told that she is blind because bricks were thrown at her, and one of the bricks hit her in her head. The blow caused severe trauma which led to her blindness. We asked if she had any family. Well she continued, said she was pregnant . . . . and as the story continues, her father in his usual ignorance, ran after her, overpowered her and beat her with intense force. She had a bad fall which caused her to have a miscarriage of the unborn fetus. Due to her handicap now, the bad boys mock her, urinates on her, punches her in the face and hurl stool at her. Every day, she begs to have her life taken. But she lives on. We asked for her husband. She had neither husband nor any known family members. We asked if she had any possessions. This was shocking because she was once married but her husband died and left her the house. Immediately after his death, young people of questionable character moved in supposedly as renters and kicked her out of her own home ultimately. Apparently these people we learned later are drug dealers and prostitutes who decided to take over her house and not pay rent to her.

After hearing this story, we could not sit by. It was important for us as missionaries to go. We wanted to go immediately! So on Wednesday morning we decided to take this urgent trip to a place where we had no idea of the location. But we went nevertheless. A few of the young girls who had befriended us came along with me, Evangelist Morris and Missionary Eve, and our beloved little Dennis. God had blessed us so much so that he was never sick not even for a day, in spite of the disaster from the hurricane. However, as we approached the home or shanty or shack whatever we saw sent chills all over our bodies. We could not believe our eyes. We saw a house and strategically placed facing the house was a "thing". Many females again of questionable character, men also of questionable character, hoodlums, punks, for that is who they are, according to their behavioral appearance, were there just standing by. The structure that we saw was like a hand-made out-house or a chicken coop, with no covering only what appeared to be old corrugated zinc which had blown off during the hurricane. The little girl who had reported this travesty to us told us that her name is "Miss Gwen". So we called out her name. She was scared and would not respond to us. We announced, "Miss Gwen, we are missionaries from America who have come to see about you." She reluctantly opened the makeshift hatch, and what we saw was horrific. We saw an old woman soaked in filth and urine. Her hair was nappy and matted. He skin was wrinkled and paper thin. She sat upright in a tight hot oven-like place on a mattress with no sheets on it. Her nails looked like that of a wild animal. Her feet were black and her nails curled over about an inch on each toe. To describe her toenails they looked like that of a big wild dog. He finger nails were no better. The place was stinking and reeked from filth, urine and garbage. This, animal-liked old woman begged to die. We again told her our names. We did not scorn her, and Evangelist Morris held her on her wrist—not her hand—and asked her what happened to her. She began to pant like a dog and tears rolled down her tightly shut eyes. We asked her if she was blind and she answered is by saying "Yes Ma-am". The tenants apparently those young people had spitefully threw bricks and hit her purposefully in her head. Because of the head trauma, she fell blind. Occasionally they would come at her and tease her and poked at her like an animal in a cage. "They beat me Ma-am". "Mek me hurry up and ded nuh"? This old woman begged to die. I could not take the stench any longer, so I moved away. But the Lord said, "NOT SO!. The old woman rambled on. We asked her from what religion is she affiliated. She said Seventh Day Adventist. We asked her if she knew the Lord, and she said "Yes." We offered to pray for her and as we began to pray, something happened. She smiled. I told her that the color of her dress was green. By now Miss Gwen felt comfortable enough with us that she began to volunteer information. Apparently, she was still in her right mind. She just cried a lot.

A little variety store was situated directly across the street. It was such a hot day so we left her alone for a few minute to go inside the store. Once inside, we asked the shop-keeper if he knew anything that was going on across the street. He said yes. He didn't hesitate to offer his input. He said he is a Christian as well and that he tried to stop the situation each time it occurs. He said he even offered to help but is prevented by the so-called "bad-boy tenants". We asked if he had anything cold to drink. There was cold water for sale. Thank God. We paid JA$70.00 for a bottle of water, which is about US$1.25. Not bad I thought under the circumstances. This store had a stand-by generator so some things were still cold. As I put the cold liquid to my mouth, it was only about four cherished sips that the Lord rebuked me again. **NOT SO!** Said the Lord for the second time. In obedience, I immediately removed the cold water from my mouth. Yes! It was a very hot day but I must be in obedience, someone needed the water more than me. So I walked across the street, knocked on the shack door and announced myself again to Miss Gwen. The old woman opened the zinc door. When I saw her I immediately put the bottle to her mouth. She drank from it like she never had water in her lifetime. I said, "Not so fast Maam, "because you may get cramps". She may not have had water in a very long time, much more cold water. She locked the zinc door right away, because she heard a familiar voice which made her felt afraid. The man was the "drug Don." He came over to me and said he needed prayer too. He demanded that I pray for him too. He identified us to be Jehovah Witnesses. I said no, I am not affiliated with that particular religion, but we are Pentecostal missionaries and are witnesses of Christ. He became sarcastic, and again demanded belligerently and with hateful antagonism that I pray for him alone at the back of the house, because he didn't like crowds. But with wisdom, I said, let us go to pray with the other missionaries. Because he was already agitated, and not knowing what he would do next. The Lord intervened. I said to the don, "Do you see those two big men standing next to me? He became confused, because I didn't think he realized that I was referring to Jesus on my right hand and the Angel Michael on the left hand. Thank you Jesus! Michael the Archangel was ready to fight for me. I was so protected. So I left without being tempted by the devil. I looked again from across the street and all I could see were bad men and women looking at us in dismay holding on to each other as though they were afraid to even make a sudden move. We left in total wonder at how God had protected us. He had protected me. We took the short way back to the mission which was about a three miles walk. Upon arriving at the mission, we began to tell of our ordeal. The bishops' wife listened attentively and then finally spoke. She said to us, "Do you all realize where it was that you all went?" We said "No". She said, "It must have been God walking directly with you all because that is the worst and most dangerous neighborhood in all of Clarendon. No one dares to even go down there. That's where the drug lords and dons are located. Prostitutes and dealers are there. You were in the lion's mouth. God bless you all". "He made a way for you all to escape out of there safe. God bless you all" . . . she continued.

We really didn't know the danger of where we had been but as missionaries it was our duty to go where the Lord send us even if it is in the lions mouth. We knew that if He sent us, He would protect us. The Bible said, "*Though*

I walk through the valley of the shadow of death, I will fear no evil for thou are with me. Thy rod and thy staff, they comfort me. Psalm 23:4

Whew! It's a hot day. Fasting service was still underway. The women were in the upper room. Wilson Hall is where the meetings were held because the Church was damaged due to the vicious hurricane. After the meeting was concluded, we were served bowls of hot soup made from goat's head and the goats' intestines. Sound gross, but quite delicious. Curried goat stew over white rice and fresh tomatoes was served as well. The day dragged on very slowly, and I was still feeling sick, lethargic, tired and weary. Hallelujah, chipped ice. A truck had delivered ice. We had ice. Not a lot, but ice. This lit my countenance immediately. I wrapped small pieces over my damp washcloth and passed it delightfully over my face. Oooh! Aaah! I gave a sigh of relief.

So evening was coming soon. I was getting very resentful of evening time because there was still no power to provide light. I had a small emergency flashlight that pastor had given me before we left, and as he said, "just in case". It came in so handy, but the batteries were running low. Still there was no running water. Someone had reported that some of the people in nearby towns said water and power would be restored in about two weeks. This was very discouraging. Nevertheless, and no matter, I was going home in one day's time. So, while it was still day time, I would pack up my luggage. The bishop said I could go to the general office and make the arrangements. I did just that. The secretary seemed to be cold, unfriendly and aloof. Her persona did not reflect a child of God, with love for a visitor. She spoke down to me as if to show that she is in control and I have invaded her space. Her countenance appeared to be one who is resentful of another. I was a little disappointed but that did not move me because I remember how the scripture said, "we entertain angels unaware, so we must be careful." Everyone else was very nice to us. I had gotten to know and love them for that. They were so helpful and willing. Upstairs now and back in my dorm room, I began putting my things away. Some of the little personal things, I had given away to a young girl who had acted as our tour guide. I sat my traveling clothes aside as well. Because we were told that we would be leaving at 2:00a.m. Thursday morning, I had to hurry before darkness came. Going home was all that really mattered. Hallelujah!

As sunset came and the evening grew even darker, dinner finished as well, I excused myself and went to freshen up for traveling the next morning. Apparently, there was another bucket of water delivered into our hallway. Thank God. This bucked was to be shared for the five people in our area. I took my small portion and brushed my teeth and freshened up as best as I could. Haven't taken a shower for five days already, since Sunday Morning at 5:30a.m., and a sweet refreshing one since Saturday August 18th. Now, what a delight it is to have even a drop of water rolled down my chest. It's amazing how a person can adjust to certain adverse conditions. You do what you have to do. The bishop and his wife invited me to their suite later in the evening after I had freshened up. We had casual conversation about trivial things. We spoke of our ministry in Florida and our own Pastors' love for the ministry. We spoke about the ups and downs of ministry life in general. Finally we spoke about us going home. We were all invited to prayer again. There was a large lit candle across from the bishops' suite. After prayer we said our good-byes and the bishop gave us gifts of native non-perishable dishes to take back home. Breadfruits were roasted for us, and Ackee in large bowls was prepared securely for traveling. I didn't sleep. I stayed awake all night, because it was very hot. They said the temperature was 102 degrees. It was very humid, because the rotted vegetative debris still ranked over in the gullies. It seemed as though only us missionaries perspired so to speak. Dennis poured bubbles of perspiration. Frankly, we were all miserable. But we didn't lose hope. We still trusted God. The people never ceased to praise God through this whole experience. But we just sweated.

I could not sleep at all; I covered my head with a sheet like I have been doing all week. There was this mosquito which I named "pest". It wouldn't leave me alone. I was feeling irritated. How does it know where to find my ears? Why could it not buzz at my hands or feet or on somebody else? Why does it have to be always at my earlobes? Anyhow, I covered my head and tried to take a nap. Well I did for about twenty minutes. How did I know this? Because imagine having a candle already burnt to the end which is still lit after you have awakened from a nap. OH, how I needed some sleep. I am schedule to leave the mission at 2:00a.m. I actually became alert at 1:30a.m., so I hurriedly put my traveling clothes on in the barely candle lit room. Finished dressing, I walked carefully down the hall to alert my sisters in Christ it was time to get going. Eventually we were ready to leave. The chauffeurs came. They were godly men chosen for this mission to drive us to the airport, 2 hours away. They used the light from their cell phones to pave the way down a very dark and narrow staircase. I led the way behind the chauffeur's one step at a time. We finally made it to the vehicle. Again, the godly men held the light from their cell phones so we could see to get in the bus. It would have been nice to have a flashlight at that time. But since we didn't, we endured. On our way now to Kingston, two hours later, we arrived at the departure entrance, only to be welcomed by a multitude of people. Let's say over 700+, camping out on line from the night before and from even earlier than us. Folks its 4:00a.m where did all these people come from. We said bye-bye and thanked the chauffeurs and began to move our luggage and inch at a time every ten minutes. By the time we actually made it inside the terminal, over 1000 people were waiting inside there too to be checked in. This was the beginning of an ultimate chaos. Check in was on a first come first serve basis. This reminded me of a movie I watched once, where the exodus of refugees depicted in that movie was trying to flee Saigon in the early seventies. It was like a stampede. And so it was, that on the day of our departure from Kingston, I felt like I was in Saigon, trying to flee for my life. I felt frightened and vulnerable.

It was us or them; "them" describing the people who were stranded at the airport from the week before, and those who were placed on standby and just needed to get off the island. We had to move fast. We were U.S. missionaries with no help from anyone. We had large baggages. I began to feel faint and it was only 5:30 a.m. in the morning. One could only imagine. It was a hot and humid morning. There was no air-conditioning. No seats either and only four ticket agents available? Imagine the Super—bowl event. Imagine only one exit in the superdome. Imagine after the ball game is over and everyone with 100 pounds of luggage or more trying to go through one exit. Scary isn't it? This is what departure morning was like at Norman Manley Airport. Everyone was anxious. Quarrels broke out. One woman fainted right in front of me. As a missionary, I dug deep in my co-workers bags to find a tiny battery operated fan. This revived the victim for a minute. But as she tried to stand up again she fainted a second time. It so happened that I was already half way down to the ticket agent desks when I looked outside and saw that the day was dawning. We had Dennis by our side. He was a trooper. He was very patient. This was a five year old diabetic child. He was never sick neither did he show any sign of exhaustion. What a trooper he was. He never complained nor cried once.

Finally, it was about 7:00 a.m., and we at last arrived at the ticket counter. People behind us made intimidating remarks and ill gestures at us. It took a lot of pushing and shoving to finally reach this point. Evangelist Morris, our most out-spoken told the agent that we are not moving from his window. He had the audacity after all this time to tell us we are on the wrong line and at the wrong window. She said, "Don't mess with me. We are not moving. You must be joking. My son is a five year old diabetic and we have been on line since four o'clock." We all decided that we were not moving. We made him see our point of view. To change lines now we would definitely miss our plane. We rebuked him and explained that Dennis had to take his insulin immediately and after four hours, we are not moving, so he had better processed our papers. He did. Immediately! So now, we hurriedly went through the gate for Immigration processing. The agent had the impertinence to issue me a three (3) month visa pass to remain in Jamaica. A defiant spirit welled up in me so much that I said, Oh No! I won't stay. I may never get back to Florida. He stamped my passport while staring at me with disdain which read August 18 to November 17. Who me? No way Jose! Not me! I so wanted to go home and take a long hot shower and wash my hair.

Almost to the end of our ordeal we sat patiently in the waiting area. Here we are twenty minutes later on August 23. At 8:45 a.m. we are walking to the aircraft. I wanted to cry so much but as a missionary, I held on to my dignity and promised not to shame my Lord. So I kept my composure. Seated in row 23F I immediately put my seat belt on, settled in comfortably and the next thing I heard was the pilot saying "prepare for Landing." I was so happy, but sadly we had only landed in Montego-Bay. It was only a twenty minute flight, not bad because I at least had a twenty minute nap in an air-conditioned aircraft. We had to again change planes for connection to Orlando, Florida. In the process we again had to wait for another two to three hours for our connecting, Flight #81 To Orlando. I didn't mind because I was going home. Two to three hours had passed by in about ten minutes. All that time I kept my heart in prayer. I was in the aircraft again. Weary, worn, and sad, more like depressed, I stumbled once again to my seat. Hunger pangs started to remind me that I had not eaten in about 24 hours. But I fell asleep. Sleep was more important than food. The next sound I heard was the voice of our pilot saying, "Orlando is sunny and fair. Prepare for landing in five minutes."

I was so thankful to God because it is He who has brought us through that horrific ordeal. He never left our side. Through it all we learned to trust in Jesus. Though it was a difficult experience, we had to endure it. When I think of all that the Lord had been through, just for me, just for us, I had to lift my eyes to heaven and thanked God. I breathe a prayer for the Pastor. I said, Honey, I love you.

The arrival entrance was a welcoming change. I spot my own people busy at work throughout the airport in addition to Immigration officers who never looked so friendly. The American people are very blessed. They are blessed because this is a country of abundance and prosperity. With that thought I said, Lord I thank you. I wanted to kiss the ground right there and then, but I didn't. Although weary from traveling over 15 hours I resorted to giving praise to the Lord for this beautiful country all the same. I said, "Lord, thank you for giving me a chance to live in it and to call it my home. So I dedicate this scripture passage to my experience, because it was the first one that the Lord deposited in my spirit as I landed in Orlando International Airport on Thursday afternoon August 23.

Psalm 121 (KJV)

[1] I will lift up mine eyes unto the hills, from whence cometh my help.

[2] My help cometh from the LORD, which made heaven and earth.

[3] He will not suffer thy foot to be moved: he that keepeth thee will not slumber.

[4] Behold, he that keepeth Israel shall neither slumber nor sleep.

[5] The LORD is thy keeper: the LORD is thy shade upon thy right hand.

[6] The sun shall not smite thee by day, nor the moon by night.

[7] The LORD shall preserve thee from all evil: he shall preserve thy soul.

[8] The LORD shall preserve thy going out and thy coming in from this time forth, and even for evermore.

My first task after returning from this mission trip was to write the following letter to Amnesty International in Jamaica West Indies.

August 29, 200-

Amnesty International
131 Tower Street c/o IJHCR
Kingston
JAMAICA, West Indies

> . . . *"health professionals can contribute to the investigation of human rights violations in general, and torture in particular; Amnesty International has adopted the following principles for the Medical Investigation of Torture and Other Cruel, Inhuman or Degrading Treatment"* . . . . —*"working to protect human rights worldwide."*—*{Excerpt taken from the Amnesty International mission statement}*

To whom it may concern:

I am a citizen of the United States. On August 18, 200-, I led a delegation to Jamaica to participate in an annual convention of one of the church groups in Jamaica. Because of Hurricane Dean, the scheduled convention was postponed due to severe damage to the facilities, rendering lack of electricity. Therefore during the daytime, we went out into the city to visit the needy and underprivileged. Our guide told us of an elderly woman, probably 87 who was being held hostage on her own premises. She was forced to live in an outhouse covered with corrugated zinc. She is blind, and is fed urine for water and is beaten and poked at with sticks on a daily basis. These people have taken over her house by force and are living there. We as missionaries are told that whenever on-lookers see the severe abuse and call for the police, when they do arrive, the perpetrators would run away and hide.

We ask to be shown where this place was and was taken to the location in _____. The place is on _____ Street, at the end of the street going south. Immediately, in front of the alleged house is a little shop, and the owners name is "Young". In the outhouse is a woman who has the appearance of an animal. The place smells like urine and feces. She is locked up in there every day even with the heat factor of 100 degrees. This is an old woman of about 87 years old who is blind. The woman answers to the name "Miss Gwen". On the day we discovered her we prayed for her and gave her water to drink. We had no food with us, but dare not to do more because of the hoodlums who stalked and challenged us. I am back in the Unites States now, and am asking you to please check this incident out and do what you can for her. She is begging to die. If she is not dead yet, there is still hope. Because of your stated mission, cited above, I implore of you to please do the right thing and save another human life.

God Bless
Very kindly yours,
An American Evangelist

CHAPTER FIVE

Mother and Me on MOTHERS DAY

A good woman is hard to find, and worth far more than diamonds. Her husband trusts her without reserve, and never has reason to regret it. Never spiteful, she treats him generously all her life long . . . . The woman to be admired and praised is the woman who lives in the Fear-of-God. Give her everything she deserves! Festoon her life with praises!—Proverbs 31:10, 31

It was another Sunday in church. Here I am again seated at my assigned seat on the second row pew. This time, it was a special day. It was Mothers day. All the mothers young and old, new and aged would be recognized in the morning worship service. A fellowship dinner would follow and the men would put their skills to the test by serving without spilling. I thought again, what it would be like in the dining room.

As Worship service ended for the afternoon, the Pastor and I, and other ministers proceeded to the outer vestibule area where we took our places in line to shake parishioner hands and greet all who had attended church. As we shook hands, so many well wishers, and so many sentiments were being sent out from every one. Some people try to evade dealing with my handshake, so they would sneak out through another exit. Nevertheless,

Mothers day has always been a beautiful day. Everyone comes out in their special best; even those who come only once every year. I love Mothers day, because it's a time when mothers are recognized for the love they give unselfishly all year without charge.

"Mothers' Day is a holiday devoted to motherhood and expresses thanks to mothers. In the United States it is observed on the second Sunday in May" (*Encarta*). So I dedicate this chapter to my readers who are blessed to have a mother still alive today.

A little excerpt I once read said, *"A father may turn his back on his child; brothers and sisters may become inveterate enemies; husbands may desert their wives and wives their husbands. But a mother's love endures through all; in good repute, in bad repute, in the face of the world's condemnation, a mother still loves on, and still hopes that her child may turn from his evil ways, and repent; still she remembers the infant smiles that once filled her bosom with rapture, the merry laugh, the joyful shout of his childhood, the opening promise of his youth; and she can never be brought to think him unworthy"*.—**Washington Irving**-

The first recollection of my mom was about the time when I was 3 or 4 years old. I remembered the cake very well, being placed on the table in the verandah, and this beautiful fair skinned woman telling me that the cake was mine because it's my birthday and as she said, I am a "big girl" now. Well, back then in the fifties, people seldom celebrated birthdays in our district village. But that day, I felt special because a cake was baked.

I had never seen a cake before but my instinct told me that it was a good treat. Oh the aroma. Imagine little eyes focusing on the cake on the table no further than a few inches from my nose. A woman they called Sheila Kelly as I later learned of her name as a youngster, had baked the cake so that my mom would sample it before she made the final batches. They usually baked cakes, puddings and twisted "alligator shaped" breads and other pastries for the local upcoming harvest. Today, they call it in America

"October-fest". I didn't know better, but because it was my birthday they said, things kind of fell into place. Nevertheless, I felt special. I could not get enough of the dark brown, chewy, sweet, morsel. My baby sisters ate their little bit as well not failing to have it all over their cheeks and bibs. In fact, everyone had some cake. A slice of cake for a 4 year old was a colossal treat, but did I have some cake.

Shortly thereafter, my mother left us seven children to relocate to the U.K. to live with our father. She left my three older brothers, my older sister, me and my two younger sisters. My older sister was living with my Aunt at that time in another town. Only then I didn't know her. But most fathers had chosen to live in England in those days primarily to seek suitable employment in order to support their families back home in the little Island of Jamaica. Jamaica was still governed by England until August 6, 1962; the day Jamaica gained its independence from Great Britain. But as a child, time was eternity. The next time I saw my mother again I would be about 9 years old. Much older now, I recalled the face of this beautiful woman, more striking than I had ever imagined, or even remembered. She had returned from the U.K. I noticed in great detail, how her complexion was white and so soft to the touch. Her silky flowing black hair with many curls, they were so soft, so attention-grabbing. Her features held my interest for so long. I knew she noticed my stares but she let me touched her all I wanted. Her lips were so pink and defined. I have never seen a woman with pink lips before, because as a child growing up in a village, women seldom improved or enhance themselves to look better. In fact, most if not all the women who lived in our village district were dark brown skinned toned, therefore portraying the same color lips. I would observe these women working in sun from dawn till dusk. The men who never traveled to England, nor held city or professional jobs such as the local elementary school teachers or post office workers, left for the fields and the women tended to their many domestic responsibilities. Most had hard calloused hands, and un-manicured nails. I observed unkempt hair many tied with a bandana type scarf, or either some would have a straw hat covering their unkempt hair. If you would notice closely like I did, most women posed dry parched aged skin even though they weren't really that old, but because of severe hardship and the severity of the status-quo there, they mostly had a horrid appearance to their countenance. Their facial expression tells the story of a woman who has been neglected; one who has not shared the deep love and attention of a husband, and one who takes life as though there is nothing else to hope for.

So therefore my mother stood out in the village like the distinguished person that she was. Of course, she was well-regarded by everyone. What she said and thought was valued by every person. Her presence demanded respect in and about our district-village. She taught church choirs, fed and clothed the impoverished, advised the schoolmasters, counseled unwed mothers, settled disputes and so many other things. Business matters were often discussed under cool shade trees quite often at our home. When villagers wanted to make major decisions, they would consult with my mother. Women or men who planned to get married would bring their intended to meet my mother. I felt special among the other children because even as a young child I was respected too. I was addressed as Miss Yvonne.

We bonded again as mother and daughters, for I had two younger sisters as well. There I was taught by her to do many things that an upcoming young lady would need to know in society of proper upbringing. Proper etiquette and good manners and politeness were mandatory. Even sitting with an upright posture at the dinner table—for no slouching was allowed—to walking with a positive stance was a part of the training. I learned the proper way in which a tea cup must be held and how to sip from it without slurping. And lastly, I should not forget the proper use of handling a knife and a fork, and the use of each piece of silverware. Reading was encouraged every evening in our home as a mandated pastime. Mother made us join the local library, and once per week we had to check out several books.

I wanted to know more about where I came from, so my mother in the long run told me in my adolescent years as much as I could understand then. My question was as I asked one day, why does everyone calls us "Miss" and the other girls are not called "miss"? Mom said, "Proper young ladies must be respected. That's just the way it is". I wanted to know why our skin was shaded fair while other girls were dark. Mom said, In Jamaica, children are born with all shades of skin color from fair to dark. And that's just the way it is. Then as I grew even older, mother told me they came from a lineage of Irish people and that my beautiful grandmother left Ireland with my other two grandaunts as young women to live in Jamaica. I was told that my grandfather was Scottish and my grandma was Irish. Their profession was breeding Thoro-bred horses in Jamaica. I know now why my heart races whenever I see a beautiful horse anywhere. It's in my blood. And I actually enjoy televised horse shows as a past time hobby. After grandfather died in a train crash, and my grandmother who I briefly knew was injured in another accident as well, lifestyle was restricted, but nevertheless, my grandmother kept her stance. I remembered her hip length braided hair wrapped like a Katter turban around her temples. I remembered her prominent nose and how she let me sit on her lap when she would come to visit. I remembered her broad grin, and thin eyelids. "Mammie" was what we called her, and all I have of her now is a copy of an old cherished photo that my aunt let me have.

My mother was a woman of excellent taste, and high standards. She had several brothers and sisters who also embraced fine manners and superior principles. Nevertheless, the time came when I had to leave the local elementary school and move to a school of better choice in town. I was placed in a Catholic convent parochial school for girls in the city called Montego Bay. From there, I learned many more things as well. My education was improved. My intellectual growth was broadened. An excited thing happened to me there as well. I met my older sister Patricia there. She looked just like me, only a little older. I loved and admired her.

She had accomplished a lot and many students and the nuns as well held her in high esteem. She didn't live in the same home as we younger ones did. I found out later that my aunt who was older than my mother raised her with my other cousins. It was not for selfish reasons but primarily because my mom was always ill from her several consistent and close pregnancies. Out of love my aunt who is still alive today assisted in the raring, and as she grew up our parents allowed the living arrangements to be permanent. But the time came when we except for my older brothers and my oldest sister Patricia, had to leave the village and bid farewell to Jamaica, a place where we called home. Actually one brother was away at university in Trinidad, and another was living in Bermuda. The latter was already married.

Departure from Jamaica to the United States at the age of fifteen years old was one of the best parts of my life because it would be my first time ever to fly on an aircraft. It was intimidating. I knew deep down in my heart, that there was something more out there for me than the little village I lived in, and the town where I attended school. Sometimes I thought, was there ever hope for tomorrow. Would I have to live there and marry another farmer like the other women? But there was hope because God was watching over me.

I resided in uptown Manhattan, New York for several years, with Mom and Dad and three sisters, for there was now an addition, a baby sister born in the U.K. I attended High School and graduated in the class of 1975, and then I was enrolled in the local City University. It was then that Daddy decided to move to Brooklyn, New York. And had he not made that decision, I would not have met my husband some years later. The first thing my husband did before our courtship was to visit with my mother. She may have interrogated him regarding several things, which neither of them ever disclosed to me until this day. My father was not so impressed because he was a local guy, but he went along with the approval of my mother for reasons of his own. We married one year later but after only a year and a half into our marriage, Mother passed away, and went home to be with the Lord. This was quite bewildering for me, because as a newly-wed, a new wife, and a new mother all wrapped in one inexperienced innocent bundle, I needed mother the most to still guide me in things that matters most to me.

The first Mother's Day after her untimely death, I visited the Hallmarks Shoppe to pick out my usual Mother's Day card for her. There is where I realized I could no longer send her the card because she was gone from my life forever. I cried, and then some more, because I missed her so much. We had become very close. I missed so many things about her. I bought the card nonetheless but never send it. It's been over 28 years now, and it seems like only yesterday that we shared so many funny and silly stories really about nothing.

So as I reflect upon this day which we call Mothers Day, I want to encourage those of you who share the beauty of having a loving mother around you. Cherish her. Care for her. Surprise her occasionally. Get to know her better. Learn all you can from her, for she is wiser than you are. According to the book of Job 12:12a, the Bible said in part . . . "*Wisdom is found among the aged*". So therefore my recommendation is for us to appreciate everything about our mother, even her shortcomings because those are which helps to mold us into what we are today. Mothers are our first teachers. Make time for her because one day she will be gone home to be with the Lord like my mother did. My time with her was very short. I was a very young woman when she passed away. A mere child-woman I was. Do not take yours for granted for she is a special gift, especially if she is a godly woman. And so, I dedicate this poem written by Temple Bailey to all mothers today to which I could not have said it any better:

-A Mother' Poem-

She taught me the pure meaning of Love
And to thank the Lord above
She taught me to catch butterflies
She taught me to admire roses
She used to kiss away my fears
And hug away my woes
She tended a beautiful garden, a garden of the heart
She planted all the good things that gave my life its start.
A chef while baking me a cake
A doctor when tending me my cold
I wonder what she couldn't do,
As I kept growing old.
A tailor, A chauffeur, a fairy god-mother at times
But never too busy for a child's nursery rhymes
She is what she was and could be none other
My sweetest angel, she is my mother.—**Temple Bailey**

Mother and me had she been alive today we would have made a great team. I love, cherish, and will always hold her memory in my every heartbeat always. And so every year as we approach the day designated to all mothers, I will never cease to remember the joy I once shared with my own, the late Ruth Evadnie Tennant—Williams, 1926-1980.

CHAPTER SIX

God Chastens Those He Loves

"But when He, the Spirit of truth, comes, He will guide you into all truth. He will not speak on his own; He will speak only what He hears, and He will tell you what is yet to come."—John 16:13

Another Sunday Morning at church, and here I am being escorted once again to my assigned seat at the second row pew by the usher. It was a beautiful day. There were beautiful faces to see again. Mostly everyone were smiling and eagerly awaiting the start of the service. Some were kneeling in prayer. Others hurried about to get a good seat. I was a little troubled and I decided that I would not walk in the procession. The usher at my bidding escorted me to my seat.

As I sat in my seat, I bowed my head and began to contemplate on why I was so troubled. Things were not going as I thought. After all I am living in a new house. How many people have the opportunity to live in a house such as mine? But yet I was not happy. I just thought and thought and thought where I could have gone wrong. Of course I knew. God chastens those who He loves. The Lord reminded me that he was chastising me because I was disobedient. There were so many alternatives of me being disobedient. I fit the glove in all of them. I was noncompliant to the word of God. I was self-willed and dissenting. As I said no one would know because I did not deliberately express myself as a defiant person. Do you know that if a believer professes to know the Word of God and do not comply to it, he is worse than firewood fit to be thrown in the fire and be burnt. Well that's where I was in my life at one time. Many of us do not confess our sins. But to do it, is healthy, and burdens are lifted. The Scripture spoke of many Bible Patriarchs who were disobedient and God had to step in as the loving father that He is and chastise that a one. Today, He is still in the chastening business. I was chastened by his right hand to uprightness. Let no one deceive you with empty words, for because of such things God's wrath comes on those who are disobedient. At one time we were in darkness, but now we are light in the Lord. So it is that we are to live as children of light for the light consists in all goodness, righteousness and truth and such things pleases the Lord. We are to have nothing to do with the fruitless deeds of darkness, but rather expose them. For it is shameful even to mention what the disobedient do in secret. But everything exposed by the light becomes visible this is why it is said . . . . Wake up, O sleeper rise from the dead, and Christ will shine on you. I came to myself one day after I heard the sermon preached about the hand of God's wrath. I repented of my selfishness right where I was seated, and I asked the Lord to forgive me. I know the Lord had forgiven me because he keeps bringing back to memory the story of his forgiveness.

And so it is that my family consisting of my husband, myself and three sons lived in the same home in Florida for about fourteen years. When the children were quite young, the house seemed so large. But, as they became teenagers, and subsequently adult children, we all crammed for space, each individual needing his own personal corner. When my sons became teenagers, we grew out of every inch of space and privacy became a luxury. But, as a still fairly young married couple, my husband and I needed and felt that the rooms were just too close in proximity. As Christians, we endured but in the flesh we all became self-conscious, especially if there was a need for intimacy. So one Saturday morning, we went looking for a home . . . "*by ourselves*". We found a subdivision close to home, work, school, shopping, and most importantly, the church, where my husband is the Pastor of a growing ministry. This was perfect. Several days later, we deposited a $1,000.00 down-payment on the home-site unto which we would build our new home. We continued looking, nevertheless, we found our dream home, or so we thought. It was located into a very upscale neighborhood like only Yes! It glittered and reflected the images of all the beauty and splendor of its amenities. The model homes were like mansions. Again, light-hearted, we placed a $3,000.00 down-payment on a home that was almost completed. The financing for the mortgage on the vacant lot was approved to build a larger home, and the financing on the mortgage for the house already under construction was approved as well. That is when the problems began. This would be the beginning of God showing us how disobedient and selfish we both were. After all, we were bible believing, born again, sanctified Christians. We had not gone to Jesus first. We went alone. We never took God along. He said he would never leave us neither would He forsake us, yet in this a most important decision, we never asked God for help.

Well, just for being disobedient, we lost the first $1,000.00 which was placed on the first home-site. Eventually, the time came when the 2nd home was completed and we moved in. It was the most beautiful home I have ever owned. We went through all the traditional ceremonies, like having people over to pray with us as we blessed the house. After we settled in, something horrid and disgusting began to take place. We found out that we were not happy after all. We were happier in the smaller house. God had not chosen for us. We chose for ourselves. Our plan was not Gods plan. God never gave us His approval to live in that neighborhood. All this time I never mentioned that God would find us a home. No. he was not a part of our plan, although there was a sense of pride of owning real estate in such an aristocratic neighborhood, we still were not happy. The devil had visited us.

We fought each other over trivial things. The family argued over non-essential matters. We began to resent each other. Screaming and discord found its way into our Christian home. Sickness, pain and much suffering came too. This had never happened before. We smiled on the outside, but silently we cried inside even at the church and at work. No one knew. I would look over at our sons, and knew that the day before, they were verbally abused, and I knew how heartbroken they are. But God bless their resilience. They never showed any outward signs of unhappiness. I sang heartily, and taught Sunday school like normal. I played the organ under the anointing, and my husband preached and people accepted the Lord. I found joy in going to church, but I regretted the time when I had to go home. We were very quiet at home among ourselves. We ate in silence and even watched television in silence. The children began to stay out with their friends a lot. I believed more and more frequent and it showed. Things were just not the same. One son moved out to live with other friends. Things were just shifting to a different way of life for us and I didn't like it. My loving husband of many years found it better not to say anything to me. He had other people who he enjoyed talking to. I resented that, and that which resulted in disagreements as well. And I remembered one day as we did our routine evening walk, also in silence, a portion of scripture which said "the Lord would not allow more on us than what we can bear."

I woke one morning and began to pray. As I prayed, God revealed to me that we were living in a place which the Lord had not given to us. And so as we sat in our back lanai one crisp fall evening before the Thanksgiving weekend, we deliberated silently over what we had done. We came to ourselves, like the prodigal son and daughter, and asked God for permission to place the house on the market for sale. The house stayed on the market for seven months. During that time we asked the Lord to forgive us of our selfishness, to forgive us for the mess that we had brought on to ourselves and to provide us with a home of his choice. We asked the Lord to show us where He wanted us to live. And we then left it into His hands for him to work out all the details.

We looked into several neighborhoods and after three home possibilities, on a sunny spring day, while sitting at my desk at work, I received a phone call. It was my husband. He sounded very excited, and relieved like a burden has been lifted from off his shoulders. He sounded like God had spoken to him. O how I recognize that special voice. It's a deliberate light aired pitch hidden in his voice. He sounded very confident. He said that he had found the house; and that he believed this is where the Lord wanted him to be. That's all he said other than I should drive by in the afternoon at lunch time and just take a look at the address he would give to me.

He had given me very precise directions. I went to the place and it was exactly where we first had went three years before. The very place where we lost the first $1,000.00 deposit, except it was the house immediately across the street from where we had previously chosen. This was situated on the right side of the street. Well now I see the hands of God working in our favor. Three years before, we had looked at this lot. It was the most expensive lot for sale in the 40-home gated community. The people apparently who had been looking into the prospect of purchasing the home-site probably couldn't afford it so it remained unsold. The developers referred to the site as the "premier lot" of the neighborhood. It was situated immediately on the water front, which is why we had originally chosen the opposite lot across the street. But you see on that day three years ago, we went looking on our own.

And so as I drove by the home and slowed down by the realtor's sign in total amazement, I thought, "Well, this couldn't be." It just can't be. This was the same lot we had looked at over three years ago. My mouth went dry. I drove back to my office and called my husband. We both decided to call the Realtor to schedule an appointment for a walk-through. Well we did. Only, we had no idea that the house was selling for a quarter of a million dollars. Houses were not selling for that of a high price tag at that period of time. Houses in the area were topped off at about $185,000.00. But this one was extremely high-priced. Did I say quarter of a million dollars? Yes I certainly did. We prayed this time. We brought the situation before the Lord and placed it into His hands. We asked the Lord to let His will be done. We thanked Him for His decision for us in this particular state of affairs. And as we drove to the house on an early February morning to meet our appointment we recognized that as Christian leaders we could never allow ourselves to make another mistake like the one we were currently in and about to get out of.

On that morning as I rang the door bell to the house for sale, I heard the melodious chimes, and an anxious feeling came over me. I never owned a house with chimed doorbells before. So I humbled myself before the Lord Why? Because my income was hardly in the range of buying a quarter million dollar home, it wouldn't add up. I continued to pray silently and ask the Lord to guide every move we make. Seated at the table, the men spoke, and discussed the business end of this transaction, while I sat in pondering silence. Then there was a different silence. All I could hear over the broken stillness was a thin voice from my mouth saying . . . . "I'll take it . . . Honey, this is the house". There was calm again. We found ourselves leaving the house and feeling very positive. We, along with the Realtor headed back to our home because the agent said in order to secure the house from other buyers, we would need an immediate deposit. My husband and I said, spontaneously, O.K., and, upon arriving home, we wrote a check for $3,000.00 to be held in escrow. I experienced finally the difference in what it felt like to have the Lord directing us in our situation. And so the work of total trust and dependence in God began. We cried and hugged each other after the Realtor left, thanked God for His direction in our lives and stood still to watch Him work for us.

From that day in February until the day of closing the title, I prayed 3 to 4 times a day for this situation. I already knew that the Lord had blessed us with this home. And so I thanked him for it again and again. I prayed affirmation prayers. I never ceased praying. I prayed the same prayer every day sometimes as many as six times. And so, one night an amazing thing happened to me as I drove home from choir rehearsals. I was listening to the anointing songs being played on my favorite Christian radio station. As I was about to pass the subdivision where the Lord was directing us to live, and I usually pause from whatever I am humming, singing, or listening to, just to repeat my simple affirmation prayer. But this time approximately 10:15 p.m., while listening to the radio, a voice, not the voice of the radio host, but a voice like one you would never hear again, a thundering voice with utmost clarity, an audible voice, spoke to me. The voice said aloud, "**IT IS YOURS!**" Now when you hear the voice of the Lord, you will recognize it. I immediately understood what had happened. I had not yet reached the place where I could say, "Lord I thank you for my house at "*whatever the address was*" . . . because before I could even prepare my thoughts to say this usual prayer of faith, the Lord had answered me. He interrupted my thoughts and said to me, "IT IS YOURS." I shouted Hallelujah, hallelujah . . . . and cried all the way home. It was another ten miles to go. I cried and thanked and praised the Lord. The voice confirmed that God had put His divine approval on the new house and he was going to work out the finances and any other detail involved in purchasing the new home. This was a home with the stamp of approval from the Lord. This was a home which had everything anyone would want in a home. It had all the niceties of just what we have always wanted. It had a three car extended garage, a nine car driveway with a gazebo at the end of the driveway. A great backyard overlooking water which strategically surrounded the parameters of the house, a heated swimming pool with an extended lanai, and island kitchen, solid oak cabinets, kitchen office, intercom system with built in surround stereo sound system, chimed doorbell, a storage attic, a study for pastor, more bedrooms and his and her bathroom, High ceilings with fans in every room, All sorts of impressive landscaping, and no home in my backyard which was an added bonus.

I said Lord, "I will dedicate this house unto your holy name". The Lord began to speak to my heart. He said to me, I was there all the time. From the beginning, I was there. Even when you both decided to go without my approval, I was there. I was there when you were both unhappy. That's when I was chastising you. That's when I was trying to get your attention. I was there when you lost money because I had greater things planned for you. All you had to do from the beginning was to make your request known to me. All you had to do was to take your burden to me.

And as we continued to pray each day, we became more and more happy. We prayed for our situation and our circumstances. We put everything before the Lord. The financing were falling into place. We came up with over $35,000.00 of our own money to complete our financial obligations to the title company. This was money we didn't even realize we had. Resources that the Lord had tucked safely away in several places were gathered together. Another amazing thing happened. The current home was still not sold. One day, we received a call from an investor who stated that he wanted to lease our home. We thought it to be untrue. Since we had multiple listing, anyone could have found our home for sale on the internet. But we trusted the Lord to lead us and He did. After we spoke to the investor, he offered to pay us $10,000.00 up front, pay our monthly mortgage installment, insurance, assessments and taxes, and pay us even more at the end of the two year lease. This is over and beyond the equivalent of what we would have paid the real estate agent to sell our home. This was money in our pockets instead of out of our pockets. Also, at the end of the Lease the investor would satisfy our mortgage with the bank. Now was God working in our favor or not. This is the favor of God. We looked over the contract, and thanked God for raising and sending a perfect stranger out of nowhere to make us this air-tight offer. We fired the Real estate agent, and entered into this lease option. Moving day eventually came, and we were happier than ever.

The Lord was working 24/7. He was working for us, and all we had to do was to trust him. We did not want to make any more decisions without putting God first. I know first handed what it means when the Bible say "who the Lord loves He chastens". Psalm 37:4 declares, "Delight thyself also in the Lord; and He shall give you the desires of thy heart."

So as I sat and listened to the remainder of the sermon, I thanked God for his love towards me and my family. I was being selfish in that I had no reason to have an unpleasant looking countenance. God dealt with me and all I had to do was to accept it, deal with it and get over it instead of having my heart troubled. I see now why the bible said, " . . . for whom the **Lord** loveth he **chasteneth**" [Hebrews 12:6aKJV]. In other words, the Lord disciplines those He loves. Jesus loves me this I know for the Bible tells me so.

CHAPTER SEVEN

Critical Transgressions

"But when He, the Spirit of truth, comes, He will guide you into all truth. He will not speak on his own; He will speak only what He hears, and He will tell you what is yet to come."—John 16:13

The Pastor rose from his seat to introduce the speaker of the hour. While I sat in my assigned place in the second row pew, the messenger waited patiently while his list of accomplishments was read. Quite lengthy I thought, so I hope with the accolade placed on his shoulder he would produce a powerful sermon. The congregation was so ready. However, not wanting to be critical, I waited just like the others who were seated as well, for the queue to stand as the messenger was announced to take his place at the pulpit. I love to hear the word of God preached. It is as though I can picture the Lord seated on His throne, high and lifted up. Isaiah said he saw the Lord in the year that King Uzziah died. So with this mental picture I eagerly wait to hear a word from God. With Bible in hand, journal, pen and a highlighter, I waited patiently and stood as the messenger proceeded to the podium. We sat at the signal of the pastor.

Prior to praying for the Lords anointing over the message and in asking the Lord for guidance to deliver it, the preacher again, proceeded to remind the congregation about himself. He told of his accomplishments, and all the stories which surrounded his life. He told us of the many people who had come to know Christ through his ministry. He told of the articles written about him in several newspapers, and the important people he had met. He told of the judges and the celebrities on Major T.V. Network who he is friendly with; he told of the accomplishment of his many sons, and up until now the message had not been delivered, and the time was already far spent.

In retrospect, I believe a spirit filled leader will do his best to promote God and not himself or herself as a matter of fact. I believe all glory and honor belongs to God. A good minister, I believe is not only spirit-filled but spirit-led. Jesus Christ stated in John 16: 13 KJV—"Howbeit when he, the Spirit of truth is come, he will guide you into all truth; for he shall *NOT SPEAK OF HIMSELF*; but whatsoever he shall hear, that shall he speak; and he will show you the things to come." Some people had begun to leave quietly, and guardedly, but the messenger didn't seem to have taken any notice that he had already lose the audience. Then I thought again, this minister is not guided by the Spirit of God, with words of wisdom. His expressions were not brought into subjection before God for direction. Because of this I felt sorry for the situation, so I bowed my head and closed my eyes, since I was feeling exhausted and possibly weary. As a Pastors wife, I cannot externalize my thoughts. A simple sign of repugnance may alert those seated around me. "Are you O.K, First Lady"? Someone tapped me anyhow, and whispered in my ears. In response, I said, "I'm O.K". So I have to be very guarded about my feelings at all times. It's as though most eyes are fixed upon me for the slightest inconsistency in my mannerism. Nevertheless I closed my eyes again and began to pray for the situation. I opened them another time and the Pastors eyes were fixed with mine and together we knew he had lost his bearings at the pulpit. It's as though we knew what the other was thinking. Our Pastor is a very wise man. We have been married for over 30 years and we are able to skillfully read each other's thoughts. So it was a special service for the men's ministry, and the men of the Church

wanted to invite a guest speaker for the day. After looking through the list
of preachers that are friends of our ministry, they came up with a minister
from "Up North" from one of the tri state areas. He was a very likable person,
very articulate and most importantly, several of the men knew him, especially
our Pastor. So this was a good reference. Only, my position is let the word
speak for you. I was instantly reminded of the scripture which said : "*And
whosoever shall exalt himself shall be abased; and he that shall humble himself
shall be exalted.*(Matthew 23:12 and Luke 14:11 KJV). I interceded to the
Lord right then for the sake of those who came to hear a Word from the
Lord. Sunday school was excellent. Praise and Worship was spirit filled. The
Choir sang like angels so now we waited. I knew that some were probably
impressed, but I was feeling anxious. I really wanted to hear from God. The
Lord was listening to me. He said six things I do hate. But I hate so many
others. Search the scriptures for them and abhor them: I suddenly began
to leaf through my bible. The first passage that I found was taken from
Proverbs 6:15-21KJV. It said, "Therefore shall his calamity come suddenly;
suddenly shall he be broken without remedy. [16]These six things doth the
LORD hate: yea, seven are an abomination unto him: [17]A proud look, a
lying tongue, and hands that shed innocent blood, [18]An heart that deviseth
wicked imaginations, feet that be swift in running to mischief, [19]A false
witness that speaketh lies, and he that soweth discord among brethren. [20]My
son, keep thy father's commandment, and forsake not the law of thy mother:
[21]Bind them continually upon thine heart, and tie them about thy neck.

The verse that was discerned to me was verse 19a. It said "A false witness
that speaketh lies". That's it. Sometimes we say things about ourselves only to
impress those that are listening. Sometimes we try so hard for people to like
us that we say things about our self that are not true. Sometimes we try to
cover-up the fact that we really don't know what we need to know, so we make
it up. The Bible said we are nothing more than sounding brass and tinkling
cymbals. Sometimes the old folks use to call such people empty barrels

because they make the most noise. We had a minister standing in front of Gods people who was promoting himself instead of promoting and exalting God, and God was displeased. I began to scribble words of transgressions in my journal, and soon it became a project. My new special assignment was to write the things that are sinful from A to Z. Now I know why the Lord had spoken to me and said "Search the scripture for transgressions that displeases me, and abhor them". My project was a good one. As I looked at the scribbles on a daily basis in my journal, the words became more of a constant reminder for me of so many offenses in the Christian walk. I too, must be careful not to embrace them because they are dangerous offenses to my salvation. Why don't we look at them carefully and pray to God to take them away from our life because they upset Him so.

INVENTORY OF CRITICAL TRANSGRESSION

Arrogance, Argumentative, Aggravating, Anger, Backbiting, Bickering, Bitterness, Covetousness, Contempt, Contentiousness, Disobedience, Deceit, Disrespectful, Doubt, Dishonesty, Double-mindedness, Envy, Evil Speaking, Faultfinding, Guilt, Greed, Gossip, Grudging, Gluttony, Hatefulness, Hypocrisy, Idleness, Ignorance, Idolatry, Jealousy, Judgmental, Lack Of Knowledge, Killing, Lust, Lying, Laziness, Malice, Maliciousness, Murmurer, Mischievousness, Neglectfulness, Offensiveness, Oppression, Pride, Prejudice, Presumptuousness, Quick-Tempered, Rebellious, Racism, Selfishness, Self-Willed, Stealing, Spiteful, Sexual Immorality, Talebearing, Unloving, Unrighteous, Unforgiveness, Unclean, Unbelief, Vexation Spirit of, Vile, Violent, Worry, Wicked, eXtravagance.

These are a list of some of things we as Christians must be careful to not be involved with. How dangerous is the path we would travel if we embrace such things. I looked at my hands and saw that I had several shortcomings. I was being judgmental and my spirit was vexed. But the Lord said that I should search the scripture for transgressions and abhor them. That's what I thought. The first form of repentance is admitting your faults. How then could I look at the minister and evaluate him. I believed that the spirit in me bore witness that the minister saw an opportunity and seized it. He was promoting himself, and that is why he was not effective. He was not humbled by the opportunity to speak of Christ and Him crucified. That's why my spirit was grieved. I asked God to forgive me, and just then the minister quoted the scripture from where his subject would be taken. By then, his message turned out to be a very brief one. The scripture passage was the whole message. Taken from *Ecclesiastes 12:13* KJV the Bible said "*Let us hear the conclusion of the **whole** matter: Fear God, and keep his commandments: for this is the **whole duty** of **man**"*.

So then if the fear of the Lord is the beginning of wisdom, was such a person mindful of the Holy Spirit? I repeatedly asked the Lord for guidance, and asked him to help me not stand in judgment of another. I so wanted to defend Jesus. I was immediately reminded of the scripture which said according to I John 4: 1-3 "Beloved, believe not every spirit, but try the spirit and see whether they are of God: because many false prophets are gone out into the world. Hereby know ye the Spirit of God: Every spirit that confesses that Jesus Christ is come in the flesh is of God: And every spirit that confesses not that Jesus Christ is come in the flesh is not of God: and this is that spirit of antichrist, whereof ye have heard that it should come; and even now already is it in the world."

One may say he is a sincere person but sincerity will not protect such a one from the consequences of poor judgment. I believe if we want to deliver a speech, or any other form of dialogue, it has its place and its time. However if the pulpit is a place to deliver a message from God, or to bring ones heart to Christ, let it only be so. It is prudent therefore, for a believer to try the Spirit and see if it is of God?

CHAPTER EIGHT

Godly Character

"But when He, the Spirit of truth, comes, He will guide you into all truth. He will not speak on his own; He will speak only what He hears, and He will tell you what is yet to come."—John 16:13

The week before Thanksgiving was busy. People were going to and fro, in and out, trying to get themselves situated for the one day celebration that America has designated to give thanks. Thanksgiving is always the fourth Thursday of November, after which the Christmas season would officially begins. The Pastor in his address to the congregation said "It is so good that America has designated only one day for thanksgiving. But according to the Bible, it tells us to "*give thanks in everything*" always. It is an everyday prerequisite for all Christians. Every believer must give thanks every single day. 1 Thessalonians 5:18 say "*In everything **give thanks**: for this is the will of God in Christ Jesus concerning you.* The Bible is full of scripture passages that make reference to giving thanks to the Lord.

So in honor of the day pastor announced from the pulpit that he realizes so many people are out of jobs and are facing severe hardships. However "*since it is thanksgiving week,* he said, *I want to make sure that everyone has a turkey and all the trimmings at their dinner table. It is my desire that no one goes hungry.*

Now if you are certain that you cannot afford a turkey, please turn your names in to one of the ushers and they will make certain that I receive your names."

Do you know that even in churches dishonesty is found? There are those who go because of tradition, and then there are those who go because it's the right thing to do. But it is a far cry from going to church to meet God and expect God to meet us there. When we go to church for the wrong reasons, it is easy to be dishonest. The pastor said, *"if you are certain that you cannot afford a turkey".* Well at the time of the Pastors announcement a turkey would cost about $12.00 at the local grocery store, and maybe cheaper at Wal-Mart. How many people cannot afford $12.00? There are many, but it is hard to believe when a person holds himself in good standing economically and shows that he is not in need that the church would be practicing fairness in handing out a turkey to such a one. There are those who I feel would need it more. Well so many of the well-off and renowned placed their names on the list. Some did not want to hand in their names to the ushers because *"then"*, as one person said to me *"the ushers would know who I am".* So some made personal visits to the pastor office and some even visited our home. Only they didn't know that pastor wanted to see the heart and godly character of his people. He only had fifteen turkeys to hand out. And so he did. He gave turkeys and boxes of groceries from the Food drive to families who he knew could definitely not afford it but had not given in their names. He also gave to those he knew were struggling like the elderly and some mothers or fathers in the church who were unemployed. People in the community that we knew of who were having a bad time, received a turkey as well, however only one person came back and said, "Thank you pastor". Pastor wound up giving away more than over fifteen turkeys. Sometimes, it is not what we do that portrays our heart, but how we do it. Sometimes it is our heart that portrays our behavior. There is an old adage that says *"action speaks louder than words",* and I truly believe that. One may say he is sincere but sincerity will not protect such a one from the consequences of poor judgment. How can we say we love, when we rob the poor of a meal just because the meal is free? Sometimes, our motive is as dangerous as our actual deed. The same thing happens during the Easter season as well when the pastor gives away the traditional Easter buns. Some families would take home two, when others have none.

I sat at my assigned seat in the second row pew, in the thanksgiving service which was held on the Wednesday night before Thanksgiving, the thought crossed my mind again. How good and pleasant it is for brethren to dwell together. I was pleased to see my brothers and sisters coming together in such unity. Some had brought covered dishes for others. Other people had brought bags of goodies for their church friends, and it turned out to be a good evening after all. Visitors came in to church because we had announced that we would have a thanksgiving service from the Sunday before. From where I stood after the service was over, I observe the ladies hugging and some even invited singles to their homes for dinner. I was more than overjoyed. We too, the pastor and myself had invited a young single mother and her daughter to come over and fellowship with us. It turned out to be more than a regular Thanksgiving dinner, but an evening where we could share and fellowship with the many young people who had eventually gathered in our home. The Bible reminded me of Galatians 5:22 which said, *"But the fruit of the Spirit is love, joy, peace, longsuffering, gentleness, goodness, faith, meekness, temperance: against such there is no law"* Galatians 5:22KJV. On that Thanksgiving dinner feast, I witnessed the spirit of love, joy and peace. I witnessed gentleness and goodness and faith and humility at the same time. And then I thought as I stood back and observed how the young people communicated among themselves, how happy they were. That is the kind of innocent contentment that the Lord desires for His people. He wants us to shut all our problems out and fully trust him to provide for us. He wants us to take our troubles to Him and leave them with Him. He is our Jehovah-Jireh which translates to say "God is our Provider". At that moment,

I do not believe any of those young people seated in my great room, cared much about their tomorrow or the sort of bills and other schedule expenses they would face the next day. They were genuinely happy. And happiness is to know the Lord.

The day ended with great joy as we decided on dessert. But I could not help but thinking of others out there who did not have something to eat. This has always been a troublesome thought for me each year especially when I look at the kitchen counter at all the leftovers that was made. Traditionally, everyone who leaves must take a platter with them, and some fruit as well. Whatever it is, "just take it", pastor would say, and be kindly affectionate one to another with brotherly love. Pastor was always quoting some scripture in a joking way.

After everyone had left for the night, my husband popped a Christmas movie in the DVD player. That seemed interesting so we both watched it for a while. Then I had another thought. I thought well if there are critical transgressions there must be godly virtues as well. These are the virtues which would allow a Christian to walk in the light of God's word. Again I scribbled in my journal the qualities which I remember off hand which I believed would help and lead a person right in the hands of God. Although the inventory was limited not only to the virtues listed, it was a head start in the right direction.

INVENTORY OF GODLY CHARACTER

Anointed, Affectionate, Admirable, Blameless, Benevolent, Brave, Believing, Charitable, Confident, Considerate, Courageous, Discerning, Decent, Encourager, Empathetic, Forgiving, Faithful, Friendly, Gentle, Giving, Generous, Grateful, Goodness, Holiness, Honest, Humble, Happy, Helpful, Hospitable, Integrity, Just, Joyful, Kind, Loving, Merciful, Meekness,

Modest, Neighborly, Noble, Obedient, Patient, Prayerful, Peaceful, Quiet, Righteous, Respectful, Saved, Sober, Self-Control, Sympathetic, Sanctified, Selfless, Trusting, Thankful, Temperate, Truthful, Tolerant, Unwavering, Unity, Victorious, Virtuous, Vigilant, Wise, Witness, Willing, Welcoming, eXtraordinary, Zealous.

"Finally, brethren, whatsoever things are true, whatsoever things are honest, whatsoever things are just, whatsoever things are pure, whatsoever things are lovely, whatsoever things are of good report; if there be any virtue, and if there be any praise, think on these things". Philippians 4:8KJV

In Romans 5:4, ones' personal character is having the faith that comes from being experienced through suffering and persecution. I have been persecuted in so many ways. At first, the enemy tried to let me believe that I was not very well liked, because so many people showed unkind behavior towards me. It is true that some of the people who I am surrounded with are often judgmental and cruel. Once upon a time I accredited it to my race. That didn't seem to work because Christ was not accepted amongst His own people either. Another time during a banquet at church I was told that I am too perfect. I was called an elitist. I was called prissy. I was even judged during the time that I went to a missionary trip with some godly sisters. They brought back a bad report to discredit me. We ate and slept together in a confined place for so many days only to be told that I behave quite sophisticated, and the people had a hard time relating to me. I believe that sometimes many individuals who profess to be believers are careless of the words that come from their mouths. Bad choices of words do hurt others. The Bible tells us that out of the same mouth come curses and blessings. Words do hurt and words do bless. But after having a closer walk with the Lord, I discovered that it is through being persecuted like Christ was persecuted and having been beaten upon by others is what had ultimately transformed me into having a godly personal character. I attended an international convention for Churches of God last year, and on the last evening of the event, many of the pastors and bishops wives approached me, to express their admiration towards me. I did not know that I was been admired for lack of a better word because I was not there to present myself before anyone. One wife in particular, held both my hands, and whispered in my ears that she wanted what I have. She said *"there is a certain grace that overshadows you, and I want it too. Pooled with a humble spirit and grace makes you shine with a glow that shows that the Lord is upon you. I pray for that. You are elegant, and so poised and yet you show such graceful humility. I want what you have. Tell me your secret?"* I was humbled by the compliment, to which I expressed that one has to always put God first in his or her life. Second, the inner reverence towards the Lord will externalize. One must fear the Lord, and show respect for His manservant. God is the Head, and then the husband. In public, he is not merely your husband but a servant of the Lord. That's the secret and a pastor' wife must recognize that. Respect must be given to the man of God. All other conditions can wait for the privacy of the home. But in public respect and honor must be shown to the head. Driving home that night, the thoughts of the episode with this young woman flowed through my head. I thought, maybe I should have said more, but little is much when God is in it. Proverbs 18:12 (NIV) reminds me that "before his downfall a man's heart is proud, but humility comes before honor." I certainly didn't want to appear proud, because all glory must be given to the Lord.

The best definition of displaying godly character was found in a commentary I read by Matthew Henry. "It is the personal experience of God's presence when circumstances are at their worst". He said, "The patient sufferers have the greatest experience of the divine consolations, which abound as afflictions abound. It works an experience of ourselves. It is by tribulation that we make an experiment of our own sincerity." **"Matthew Henry's Commentary".** Our pastor always teaches us that "when we are at our lowest point, our truest character reveals what is really in our heart". In 1 Corinthians 15:33, character is expressed as "true companionship." In the Greek, it is expressed as steadfast and honest communication. Bad character, in contrast, is that of an ungodly person. An ungodly person is one who is disrespectful, ugly spirited, blasphemous and downright irreligious. They have no sense of spiritualism. Everyday is the same old . . . same old way of life. If it feels good, then it must be good. These are they who will sell you out with no remorse. Friends are not friends if they will sell you out for a drink, money, or take side with the enemies. Don't forget what Judas Iscariot did to Jesus. He sold him out for thirty pieces of silver. A person with godly character will risk the approval of his best friends, risk his place in social circles, and care none the less if he loses everything he owns to maintain a true relationship with the Lord. One who displays godly character is courageous and resourceful. He releases patience in his suffering and is dedicated in his love for others just as he would want others to be dedicated to him. A person of godly character places his trust completely in God.

CHAPTER NINE

The Effectual Fervent Prayer

"So do not fear, for I am with you; do not be dismayed for I am your God; I will strengthen you and help you, I will uphold you with my righteous right hand." Isaiah 41:10KJV

As a choir director for several years, my duties include leading the adult church choir, leading the women's ministry choir, being a vocalist in the praise and worship team, and being a soloist as well. I love to sing, but one would think I had formal training. On the contrary, I had no formal training. It was just another thing that I loved to do as a young person because singing was a part of our evening past time at home during our early days coming up. Singing was among the many things we did together as a family. Mom sang, and taught church choirs, and everyone eventually played an instrument; no melody was too hard for family members to just learn and harmonize. We all had great harmony and our voices blended well. Of course, my brothers sang bass, baritone, and alto, Momma sang tenor, and we the girls sang soprano. Sometimes as little girls, we were frequently invited out to sing for small church gathering. We thought nothing of it, because it was our pleasure to sing. All this amateur training developed more as I became a teenager, I sang with the "Tabaneers", a girls' choir at the church which I formerly attended. The choir consisted of about 45-50 teens. We went to places that I have never been before. So, as a Pastors wife many years later, singing and playing the church organ was expected. It seemed as though musical talent is a prerequisite for Pastors wife. I often jokingly tease my husband that we are like the Sunday special. The Church hires the pastor, and gets his wife for free. But I so love the joy it gives me and the fulfillment it brings, when those I teach who thought they didn't have a voice properly trained to sing or those who couldn't even strike a tune were now singing like some of the well known big choirs out there. In fact we have received invitations to many churches. A few of the vocalists from our choir have already had CDs to their name.

Yet, sometimes the thing we love the best are the very same thing that harms us, if it's not done in moderation. As I read the scripture from Isaiah 41 verse 10, the Holy Spirit revealed a picture of how God would cradle and comforts his child during times of uncertainties. He holds his special children up in His strong arms and cradles them like a mother cradles her newborn.

Many of my friends and church family knew that I had been ill for several weeks. I eventually reached to the point where I confessed that something was seriously wrong, and I would die. My body became lifeless to me; I wobbled with no strength under my knees; my feet dragged like I was pulling bowling balls; I lost appetite for food; and I became seriously miserable. I suffered during those times but knew spiritually that this was my dispensation. Then I remembered how pastor had taught us several weeks before in Bible Studies that God would take us through a time of testing before he elevates us. So I had to go through my purpose and with that assurance, I comforted myself. As the weeks went by, my body became more and more lifeless. I visited the doctors and they prescribed several medicines, but instead of getting better, I got worse. The worst times ever were during the nights; only if the coughing would stop.

Several months before, I began coughing, it was as though I had swallowed something the wrong way, like a sharp fish bone, and I had choked myself on it. Only, these were episodes of severe coughing which became more and more frequent. It seemed as though all I did was cough. "Something was seriously wrong", I would hear myself said, because I couldn't stop coughing. I never smoked? Yet I sounded like a person who had smokers cough. The dry, hacking uncontrollable persistent coughs not only concerned me but became disturbing to those around me. People were very polite, but I knew they were saying, "Honey, you'd better get that cough checked out". In fact one of the women in the office where I worked said the very same thing.

Well I did, and the doctor told me that I had this, and I had that, medical terminology of which made no sense to me. I had taken all the medicines the doctors had prescribed, but none helped. The church family began to pray for me. The prayed without ceasing [like the scriptures taught us], when they realized that I had started to withdraw from noon day services on Tuesdays, Wednesday Night Services, choir rehearsals, and even Sunday Evening Worship Services, where I played a essential role. I began to miss work schedules as well, but the fact was, I never missed church. Even when I didn't feel good, I would still attend church services, and played the organ too. I couldn't sing as well as I used to before, but I tried. With the terrible coughing, I admitted again that something serous had happened to me. The enemy was attacking my body. And I remembered how the Bible tells of how the devil had attacked Job's body too. I became weaker, and all I wanted to do eventually was to stay in bed, and sleep. I had no choice for the medicines made me drowsy anyhow, and I couldn't even see to read my scriptures. My eyes had become weaker and the words were looking blurry. Confined to bed now, my only activity was to meditate, pray and sleep. I had to sleep in a sitting position. I had lost my appetite and the only thing that I could barely eat was a few slices of pears and a small amount of grapes.

This was hardly anything to keep me strong, but the Lord sustained me. Then the Lord laid it on my husband's heart to take me to the emergency room. The doctor there put me through a vigorous breathing regiment to test my oxygen intake. This was a very hard test for a sick person, but they prescribed a breathing mechanism, and different medicines. As the days went by and I continued to go for breathing treatments, good air began to find its way back into my lungs, I actually began to feel better. I was lacking the oxygen all the time which had caused coughs and coupled with acid reflux entering into my lungs due to my previous sleeping habits. All these things had caused severe complications.

One night as I finally slept, the Holy Spirit ministered to me in a dream. He brought before me the STRONG HAND OF GOD holding a Bible. The scripture was taken from St. John 14:1 which said "Let not your heart be troubled; ye believe in God believe also in me." It was the voice of the Lord which spoke. As I turned to observe my surroundings, and praised God as well, I saw a co-worker that I had ministered to several months before. She appeared before me. She smiled and handed me a scroll. Then the Lord said to me again, "Read". I took the white scroll and read the words as clearly as they appeared on it . . . . "Do not be dismayed for I am with you; do not be dismayed for I am your God; I will strengthen you; and help you; I will uphold you with my righteous right hand".

This was my breakthrough. The spirit of the Lord had revived me. I woke the next day feeling refreshed. I dressed myself and went to church for it was now Sunday. The day after that I returned to work for a few hours; then the following day, I went to Noonday Fasting and Prayer service. The color had begun to appear in my cheeks. My eyes sparkled people said. The Lord's strong hand was upon me and He was upholding me. I was walking in His strength. As I arrived at work the next few days, I became so lighthearted as if a weight had been lifted from off my shoulder. My co-workers gathered around me to express their well wishes and to welcome me back to work. Of course I had only been gone a week and a half, but to them it seemed like eternity because I was always at work, except when I am out on vacation. But a strange thing occurred. The co-worker who handed me the scroll while the Lord spoke to me in my dream, was the same one who entered my office to welcome me back as well and had now handed me a little note on white paper which she insisted that I read. She said the Lord had lay upon her heart a little scripture for me to read which she know would encourage me while I recuperate. You know, I felt as though I had seen this sight happening before. Like *déjà vu.* The words read "They that wait upon the Lord shall renew their strength; they shall mount up with wings like eagles; they shall run and not be weary, they shall walk and not faint." This is what I saw in my dreams.

I truly believe the Lord had His hands upon the situation and He wanted to give me a sign to let me know that he had answered my prayers. My outlook for the remainder of the day from thereon was to always total focus on Christ. I felt such energetic walking in His strength, my faith was strengthened and my mind was fixed on what had happened over a six month period that purposed in my heart to dedicate my life to the Lord. The Holy Spirit was with me and the joy in my heart revealed it audibly.

I could hear myself at varied times repeating thanksgiving affirmations to my Lord. THANK YOU JESUS!! HELLELUJAH!! Thank you for saving me. True, those were trying and uncertain times. I called upon the Lord and I knew He heard my cry. I know that He pitied my groan. The Word of God declares that the effectual fervent prayer of a righteous man or woman availeth much. James 5:16b JKV. But I had to go through my struggles. I knew that while I was going through, the Lord was holding me in His Bosom, like a mother who cradles her newborn. Jesus cared for me and He healed me for I am His child. I said thank you Jesus for answering the effectual fervent prayer of those who had set aside that special time in their schedule to pray for me. I said thank you Jesus for healing my afflicted body. Those times of physical weakness was over. Those times of coughing were now over. My body is declared the Lords' anointed. The Lord would not allow anything to come upon me beyond what I could bear. Enough was enough! I began to declare complete healing over my body in Jesus Name. The Lord said He would uphold me with His righteous right hand, and I declared it to be so in Jesus name. He told me not to be troubled nor be dismayed for he would take care of me. And today, I am free and am healed because God said, "by His stripes, I am healed" . . . Isaiah 53:5d; and I would mount up with wings and soar like an eagle. Don't you know that when we go through the circumstances and struggles of life God is there with us? He said in His Word that He will never leave you, neither will He forsake you. Just trust Him in all His precious promises and ask Him for more faith so that when He comes He will find you with it. AMEN.

ACKNOWLEDGMENTS

To my Lord and Savior, Jesus Christ, the author and finisher of my faith, I give honor.

To my husband Barrington, any words of thanks are so inadequate, because your loving support and encouragement means so much to me. You have always encouraged me to write.

To my church family at Poinciana Pentecostal Church of God, I thank you all for your love and I encourage you to continue the work of the Lord.

To my family and friends I thank God for each of you. You are all unique in your own way.

To the staff of Xlibris Corporation, I thank you all for your enthusiasm in helping me during this project and seeing it through to the end.

My cup overflows with great joy.

Rockell Y. Brown

www.ingramcontent.com/pod-product-compliance
Lightning Source LLC
Chambersburg PA
CBHW031253280526
45784CB00004B/1835